BEYOND THE MUSIC I

C000068934

FRITZ KREISLER   Lithograph by L.X. Fanto 1932

RIKI GERARDY

BEYOND THE MUSIC LESSON

A guide to the advanced study
of a musical instrument

ZELIA
2003

First published in 2003 by
Zelia Ltd.
PO Box 437
Edgware
HA8 8ZT

Riki Gerardy's right to be identified as the author of this work
has been asserted by him in accordance with the Copyright,
Designs and Patents Act 1988

Copyright © Riki Gerardy 2003

Excerpt from Strauss: Don Quixote, copyright assigned 1932 to
CF Peters, Leipzig. Reproduced by kind permission of Peters
Edition Ltd, London.

ISBN 0-9544675-0-7

A CIP catalogue record for this book is available from
the British Library

All rights reserved. No part of this book may be reproduced or
transmitted in any form, electronic or mechanical, including
photocopy or any information storage and retrieval system,
without permission in writing from the publisher.

Typeset in 11/13pt Sabon by Cambrian Typesetters, Frimley, Surrey
Printed in Great Britain by Halstan, Amersham, Bucks.

Everyone wants to be right, but no one stops to consider if their idea of right is right.

F. M. ALEXANDER

COVER PHOTO: PABLO CASALS   Photo G.G. (Prades)

Contents

Frontispiece: Fritz Kreisler
Table of musical excerpts viii
How to read this book 1
Introduction 3
Preamble 4

PART ONE—BASICS 6
Stretching 8
Walking 10
Posture 12
Warming-up 14
Balance 16
Exercises 18
Conception 20
Production 22
Spontaneity 24
Control 26
Focus 28
Difficulties 30
Accuracy 32
Inspiration 34
Routine 36

PART TWO—HOMEWORK 38
Phrasing 40
Line 42
Information 44
Melody 46
Rubato 48
Rhythm 50
Pulse 52
Metre 54
Harmony 56
Articulation 58
Dynamics 60

PART THREE—REHEARSAL 62
Response 64
Ensemble 66
Timing 68

Tone 70
Intonation 72
Technique 74
Detail 76
Virtuosity 78
Objectivity 80
Listening 82

PART FOUR—BACKGROUND 84
Background 86
Evolution 88
Style 90
Expression 92
Drama 94
Depth 96

PART FIVE—PERFORMANCE 98
Preparation 100
Memory 102
Nerves 104
Pacing 106

PART SIX—POST MORTEM 108
Perspective 110
Problems 112
Self-confidence 114
Poise 116
Judgment 118

FURTHER THOUGHTS 120
Creativity 121
Breathing 122
Platform manner 123
The soloist 124
Conducting 127
Drawing of the author 130
Afterword 131
Appendix: Points often
    neglected 132

Musical Excerpts

Bach: Prelude in C — 5

Mahler: Symphony No.5 — 9

Mozart: Symphony No.41 — 11

Bazzini: La Ronde des Lutins — 13

Anon: Plainchant — 15

Chopin: 1st Etude — 17

Paganini: 5th Caprice — 19

Brahms: Double Concerto — 21

Schumann: Cello Concerto — 23

Kreisler: Schon Rosmarin — 25

Tchaikovsky: Symphony No.6 — 27

Liszt: Mephisto Waltz — 29

Paganini: Violin Concerto No.1 — 31

Semiquaver exercises — 33

Schubert: String Quintet — 35

Mozart: Clarinet Quintet — 37

Brahms: Piano Concerto No.1 — 41

Mozart: Symphony No.36 — 43

Dvorak: Cello Concerto — 45

Beethoven: Symphony No.2 — 47

Beethoven: Symphony No.9 — 47

Franck: Violin Sonata — 49

Brahms: Cello Sonata in E minor — 49

Mozart: Oboe Quartet — 51

Mozart: Piano Concerto in G, K453 — 53

Bach: Concerto for Oboe and Violin — 53

Mozart: Symphony No.40 — 53

Beethoven: String Quartet Op.18 No.1 — 53

Brahms: Violin Concerto — 53

Brahms: Symphony No.2 — 55

Beethoven: Symphony No.3 — 55

Mozart: Symphony No 38 — 57

Bach: St. Matthew Passion — 57

Saint-Saens: Cello Concerto No.1 — 59

Schumann: Cello Concerto — 59

Bach: Solo Violin Sonata No.1 — 61

Schubert: String Quintet — 65

Beethoven: String Quartet Op.18 No.6 — 67

Strauss: Don Quixote — 69

Harmonic Series — 71

Beethoven: String Quartet Op.18 No.4 — 73

Vieuxtemps: Violin Concerto No.4 — 75

Tchaikovsky: Rococo Variations — 77

Liszt: Un Sospiro — 79

Brahms: Hungarian Dance No.1 — 81

Beethoven: Symphony No.6 — 83

Mozart: Clarinet Concerto — 87

Beethoven: Overture—Leonore No.2 — 89

Beethoven: Overture—Leonore No.3 — 89

Boismortier: Cello Sonata Op.5 No.3 — 91

Brahms: Violin Concerto — 93

Verdi: Requiem — 95

Beethoven: Violin Concerto — 97

Mozart: Eine Kleine Nachtmusik — 101

Schumann: Piano Concerto — 103

Mozart: Serenade for Wind K361 — 105

Chopin: Polonaise in A flat — 107

Brahms: Symphony No.1 — 111

Elgar: Enigma Variations — 113

Bihari: Racoczy March — 115

Mozart: Horn Concerto No.3 — 117

Haydn: String Quartet Op.76 No.5 — 119

How to read this book

Try reading the left hand pages first. The fifty two sections give a summary of the whole subject. They contain most of the essential information which is given in greater detail on each facing page.

We do not forget how to ride a bicycle.

ANON

Take more interest in scores than in virtuosi.

ROBERT SCHUMANN

Introduction

Great music speaks directly to our hearts, across the whole range of human emotion. It is an art that depends for its existence on the performer.

Certain players know how to communicate. They magically convey to listeners the inner depth of a work. After this, other performances may not sound the same—something seems to be missing.

This is because certain qualities, that are a vital part of musical communication, are easily lost while studying technique and repertoire. It is hard to reach a high standard of playing without this happening. The mysterious loss happens through involvement with difficulties of learning—it is just a stage of development.

However fine the critical ability, it is hard to judge our own work. The shock of hearing a first attempt at recording soon passes but, even after some experience, it is not easy to know what is needed.

The way forward is to become a bit more detached, so as to see things clearly. Not impersonal—just enough to allow understanding and control, to prepare the way for more complete involvement. Then it is possible to rediscover missing qualities.

That quest is the subject of this book. The first part—how to practise more effectively, the second, third and fourth—how to progress by using our own creative abilities, the fifth and sixth—how to be in command while performing. When busy learning, it is easy to miss the obvious; there is so much to be aware of at the same time. Here, all these qualities are considered: by going deeply into the whole subject, further thought may be stimulated.

When it is clear what to do, questions become more important than answers. The well-phrased question may contain the seeds of its own answer. This leads to various directions of discovery.

Find which questions are most relevant. For these, ready-made answers will not be enough. Instead of asking how to do it, how to look at it becomes the relevant enquiry. Advice may still be sought, but progress is now self-motivated. This is the way to develop an individual voice in music.

This book is for players of any instrument. Some advice here may only relate to particular ones, but this doesn't happen very often.

Beyond the music lesson
there is a world to discover,
where music breathes, speaks and sings through us,
resonating as our natural voice.

PREAMBLE

There is not time in a music lesson to ask all our questions—especially those that cannot be discussed quickly.

Teachers often wish that there was more opportunity to share their depth of experience.

Here there is no clock, so it is possible to explore together many aspects of music making.

Many ideas here may already be known; but knowing, in its fullest sense, implies doing. Almost every musician finds that some aspects of playing come more easily than others. Real progress is made when all areas are addressed.

Remember always to breathe, to listen and to think. This saves so much time—then practice becomes creative, rather than repetitive.

J.S. Bach: The Well Tempered Clavier, Book 1, Prelude 1.

Bach begins the first of his Preludes as if he has already made the whole journey and has come back to tell us about it. We cannot add to its completeness—only try to express it.

If I don't practise for a day, I notice it;
if I don't practise for two days, the critics notice it;
if I don't practise for three days, the public notices it.

EUGENE YSAYE

The spirit will come if the Lord is willing—first you must have a body that works.

NADIA BOULANGER

PART ONE

BASICS

Making music is an activity
that comes from our whole being.

Keep contact with that wholeness
when working at details.

Practising is the time
for listening, discovering and experimenting.

Let the day begin with some gentle stretching,
much as a cat does after sleeping.

Stretching exercises energise the body,
increase flexibility
and give protection against physical stress.

STRETCHING

Athletes have warming up routines, essential for the reduction of physical stress and for bringing the body to its best level of function. They would never begin intense work without preliminary exercises involving the whole body.

Gentle stretching helps to maintain the strength and flexibility of muscles that are much used. It counteracts any contraction that may occur during long hours of work or travel. Such contraction could cause problems if allowed to build up.

Stretching will also increase energy level and general fitness. Never strain the body—never continue an exercise to the point at which it hurts. Avoid arching the back while stretching.

Stringplayers and pianists frequently have to encompass large stretches of the hand. Regular, careful work at extensions can increase the ability to encompass intervals. Consider the use of the back and the arms, not just the hands in isolation.

Mahler: Symphony No.5, 1st mov. bar 2.

The concentration of emotion calls for a freer attitude to rhythm than the traditional give and take of rubato. This is a totally different aspect of stretching—that of prolonging a melody.

The morning walk,
or any other outdoor exercise,
reconnects us with our bodies,
with nature
and with the outside world.

Make morning exercise a regular routine—
move and breathe naturally,
before beginning more specific and focussed actions
involved in playing an instrument—
it is an essential ingredient of good practice.

When working for long hours,
take exercise
between periods of intense concentration.

WALKING

Go for a walk or a jog before beginning to play in the morning. Choose, if possible, a circular route, in which a given distance must be covered.

Walking exercises and refreshes us and frees the breathing. Such general exercise is important as a further protection against physical stress in playing.

Choose also an occasional activity that will give more strenuous exercise—one that will make you slightly out of breath is ideal.

Mozart: Symphony No.41, 2nd mov. bar 5.

Only a flowing tempo will reveal the magic of this 2 bar phrase extension (bars 9–10). Find a tempo that will not make the demi-semiquavers (32nd notes) sound rushed. Bar 8 maintains the energy of bar 7, continuing the momentum into this extension.

Andante (Italian for 'going') is the tempo associated with walking speed.

Put the instrument to you—
don't put yourself to the instrument.
Use a large mirror
for occasional checks of your sitting position.

When playing, feel free to move to any position,
but always remember to return
to a point of balance.
As far as possible,
let the hands be free of supervision by the eyes.

POSTURE

Posture is not a matter of holding a certain position. It means having an overall sense of balance that enables you to move to any position and return. Without this sense of balance you might only partially return. If you look down at the movement of the hands, don't forget to come up again, or else you will remain partially crouched over the instrument. Cellists and guitarists will end up twisted to the left as well.

A sense of body balance means not being wrapped around the instrument as if there for its benefit. Position the instrument appropriately to the way you sit or stand. Pianists will need to organise themselves, rather than the instrument, but the principal is the same.

Posture and breathing are closely related. It is easy to fall into the trap of holding the breath while trying out some new and intricate manoeuvre. Breathing should be relaxed and even. The way we breathe affects our state, and we can affect our state by the way we breathe. (See p.122.)

A mirror is useful for brief diagnostic checks, but it should not be overused. When practising before a mirror, look for cause rather than effect. For example, it is pointless for a stringplayer to spend long periods in front of a mirror trying to keep the bow straight and to avoid its sliding up and down the string. Looking at the arm to examine the bowing action may reveal the cause of the problem—the movement of the bow is only the effect.

Bazzini: La Ronde des Lutins—middle section.

The burlesque nature of this passage has the violinist playing the same note on all four strings. This demonstrates how the left elbow travels in an arc so that the hand can best approach each string.

Warming up exercises on the instrument
should gently mobilise hands and arms,
without disturbing body balance
or restricting breathing.

Avoid locking shoulders, elbows or wrists,
bending over the instrument,
twisting the body unnaturally,
or making faces while playing.

WARMING-UP

Base warming-up exercises partly on current known weaknesses—movements which need greater mastery. This is the way to find balance and control more quickly. With careful choice of exercises, you can make progress right from the start of your work.

Make a personal collection of exercises, which can change according to needs. Base it on activating certain groups of muscles.

Choose which of these exercises to use when there are only a few minutes to warm-up.

Observe body balance and breathing while warming-up. Establish a pattern that can be carried forward into work on interpretation.

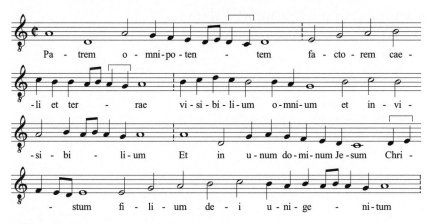

Pa - trem o - mni-po - ten - tem fa - cto - rem cae -
-li et ter - rae vi - si - bi - li-um o-mni-um et in - vi -
-si - bi - li-um Et in u-num do-mi-num Je-sum Chri -
- stum fi - li - um de - i u - ni-ge - ni-tum

Plainchant.

There is an interesting similarity between singing plainchant and warming-up on an instrument. Both need a disciplined yet free approach without any locking of the body.

Within a position
always let the hand have a sense of balance.

This comes from awareness
of the whole group of notes being played.

The use of the back and arm
is an integral part of hand balance.

BALANCE

Balance involves the whole body. Consider the balance of any part of the body from this perspective. Think of the fingering of a note in relation to the balance of the hand and arm. See which hand position relates to the notes that follow; also whether you need a close or extended grouping of the fingers. Careful orientation of the arm can smooth the progression between notes, both in a particular hand position, and in moving between positions. In this way the arms play an important role—correct functioning depends on freedom of the shoulders and good use of the back.

See how arm weight combines with direct action from the fingers. Awareness of the use of pronation (in which the palm rotates towards the floor) and supination (the palm rotates towards the ceiling) is important in the specific directing of weight and energy. Use arm weight as an alternative to pressure, but avoid becoming floppy or heavy. To use arm weight correctly, relate it to good use of the whole body.

When raising the arm sideways, allow your shoulder blade to move with it—don't hold it in. Beyond a certain height it is natural for the shoulder blade to rise with the arm. Avoid pushing the shoulders forwards or backwards, or holding them up for long periods while playing—a neutral position is preferable. Regular exercise and even breathing will help to keep the shoulders free.

The elbows are hinge joints. The forearms move in and out and can also partially rotate. Their range of movement appears larger because of the mobility of the ball and socket joint of the shoulders. Any inhibition of function in the elbow is caused by tension in the forearm and upper arm. The joints themselves do not become tense. The hands move laterally and vertically from the wrists and can rotate in either direction.

Essential movements of the hands and arms are often complex and continuous. Don't interrupt their sequence by uncontrolled body gyrations. You will not be static if you concentrate on these essential movements within an overall body balance.

Chopin: Etude No.1.
Good balance is essential when playing all 24 Etudes in one concert.

17

Limit the time you spend on technical exercises—
when you stop is as important as when you start:
in this way enjoy working at them regularly.

Technical control
comes from operating within your abilities:
scales and studies stretch capacity
and bring control.
Control is cumulative—
hence the need for daily technical exercises.

As well as acquiring facility,
develop quality of technique—
this comes from exact coordination
and awareness of every sound made.

Play scales and exercises as music
that is being prepared for performance.

EXERCISES

Use technical exercises to expand range and control on the instrument. As well as working on published collections, develop the ability to improvise exercises around specific points of technique. Try playing difficult passages in various keys and with different speeds and articulations. This needs constant attention, since there is always something to improve. If such exercises exaggerate the difficulty then, once they are mastered, the original passage will be playable.

However difficult the exercise, don't let it affect the overall balance or cause physical stress.

See exercises as music, not just finger gymnastics. Then they can bring fluidity as well as control. Work at maintaining tone quality through difficult passages, with precise rhythms.

Play regularly scales of all types, in every key, using a variety of rhythms and different fingerings. Prepare them as if for public performance, with good tone quality and evenness.

The greatest studies are a part of the concert repertoire—play the others as if to consider them for this category. Treating them as music will create the need for immaculate technique. Focus on those aspects of playing that are obvious to the listener, but less so to the player.

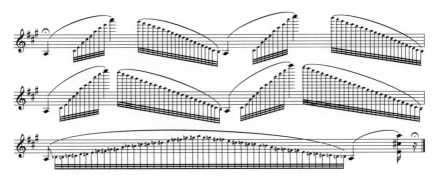

Paganini: Caprice No.5.
Scales in all forms and arpeggios are the foundation of instrumental technique.

After detailed technical work,
put down the instrument
and take up the score.

Immerse yourself in the music
away from the difficulties of the notes,
and decide how to play the piece.

Develop the ability
to hear the work in your inner ear.

CONCEPTION

Work at the score away from the instrument. Planning of interpretation is then uninterrupted by instrumental involvement. View the work as a whole, and observe how phrases relate to form the musical line.

Work at the instrument is often concentrated on coordinating physical movements. One part of the mind controls the physical function, another the interpretation. Score study develops conception and understanding.

This way of working brings a deeper contact with the structure of the music. It is like seeing a work from the inside. Subtleties of interpretation can then relate to an overall plan.

Brahms: Double Concerto, 1st mov. bar 52.

Maintain the tempo in bars 55–6. This creates momentum and shows bar 57 as beginning the real first ritornello. The listener then hears how the introductory passages lead to this point.

This is an example of how interpretation can make the structure clear. (See also mus. exx. on pp. 45 & 97.)

Returning to the instrument,
work at realising your conception.

The fingers may want to go their own way
as if they had a mind of their own—
don't let them.

Express what you have discovered—
shape of phrases,
tone colours
and the structure of the music.

PRODUCTION

Realise the conception by letting the mind and emotions direct the fingers and by letting the ears be the referees. Know what you want and work towards producing that result.

One stage is fluency and control in playing the notes, the other is training the hands to express a conception of the music. The hands always need strong direction. This is both in acquiring control and accuracy, and in shaping phrases exactly as conceived.

Schumann: Cello Concerto, 2nd mov. bar 5.

Take a slight breath between the two D sharps in bar 8. This would be a natural breathing point for a singer.

Often a short breath mid-phrase can add definition and vitality. Stringplayers, pianists etc. must learn the intimate connection between breathing and phrasing. This is best done by singing through phrases, to discover their breathing points. This ability will not be found in learning instrumental technique—it is a purely musical matter.

After finding technical control
to realise musical intentions,
play freely for a while.

In your first encounter with the work
you may have felt an openness to it
that became elusive in further study.
Those instinctive reactions
may have become somewhat modified
in refining and balancing interpretation,
but could have value
beyond logical thought.

The mind cannot go all the way—
leave space for intuition.

SPONTANEITY

After this work, play freely with energy and abandon. The logical mind can understand structure and plan interpretation, but it has its limitations.

The basic plan of expression comes from the conception. To discover finer shadings, put aside the logical approach and work with instinctive reactions and perceptions.

Go with feelings and fantasy to discover new colours and possibilities. Even if you eventually reject many of these, others may bring new dimensions of expression. Find a balance between spontaneity and control.

Kreisler: Schon Rosmarin.

The ties on the high and the low E facilitate the 2 bar metre of the waltz rhythm, by lightening the beginning of each second bar.

This example initiates understanding of metre—not easy to define (see p.54).

As a passage increases in volume and intensity
use only the necessary muscles to express it.

Reflecting the intensity elsewhere in the body
will not help tone production
but diverts or wastes energy.

Listen to the sound as it is played,
not to what you think is being produced.

CONTROL

When sitting still, though not so still as to feel rigid, good body balance can facilitate control.

Think and feel the phrase, express it through the technique and listen to the result—this is action. If the body curls up subjectively while searching for shades of expression—this is reaction. At that moment the danger is a reduction of muscular control. We may not notice this while busy with the music.

Observe whether any non-essential body movements occur each time you reach a certain place in the music. This may point to a muscular imbalance for which the body is compensating. Be aware of any involuntary movements in the mouth: this can be the result of tension in the neck or the jaw.

Tchaikovsky: Symphony No.6, 1st mov. bar 311.

Correct muscular use allows extreme dynamics without undue effort or strain.

To learn fast—work slowly.
Focus on technical passages
so as to programme the fingers for accuracy.

At a slow speed
eliminate any weakness of rhythm;
give attention
to articulation, intonation,
accuracy and tone quality.

Solve any problems
by considering in detail
the movement from one note to the next.

FOCUS

At a slow speed, it is easier to understand and memorise the correct sequence of movements. Play accurately and rhythmically—then the gradual increase in speed to the normal tempo is not a problem.

Try out fingerings in tempo, since what works well when played slowly may not be suitable at speed. When working slowly, relate movements, as far as possible, to those that will be used at the correct tempo—for example, use the same amount of bow.

Liszt: Mephisto Waltz, bar 27 of penultimate Presto section.

A passage that benefits from slow work, to plan precise movements.

If there are difficulties with a passage,
avoid frustration
by examining the nature of the problem.

Decide exactly how the passage should sound
then, while playing, consider its timing,
checking that all notes receive their full value
and that the ends of bars are not hurried.
Play very slowly and calmly,
consciously broadening short notes
and not hurrying from one note to the next.

Divide the passage into sections,
finding economic ways
to move between the notes—
sometimes another fingering can help.
When there is a particular difficulty,
decide which muscles should make the movement.
On finding a comfortable way
play slowly, to affirm complete control,
then gradually increase the speed.

Practise each section separately
then begin to put them together,
with a slight break between each section.
Shorten the breaks as the speed increases
until the passage flows naturally
and there is control.

DIFFICULTIES

If a passage is causing problems, devise a routine to meet the situation. Clarity of thought is necessary to analyse the passage calmly. The mind needs to slow down so that the sequence of movements can be reworked at a very slow speed. Often a change of fingering or technical approach can make a difference, but avoid changing fingerings just before a performance.

Divide the passage into small groups of notes. Pause between each group, remaining still and calm for a few seconds. Make pauses also before notes reached by difficult movements or changes of position, so as to have time to gauge the distance. Finish each group—make the difficult movement, stay still and then play the next notes. The next stage is gradually to shorten these pauses until they are inaudible, while retaining a sense of calm as their length diminishes. Be aware of exactly how you want the passage to sound.

If the passage is still not right, leave it and come back to it the next day. This is the way to avoid muscular or mental fatigue. Sometimes problems diminish or disappear overnight, perhaps through the workings of the subconscious mind.

When studying a long, technically demanding work, start practising from various places on different days. Then, if a section is exhausting, the succeeding passage will not be associated with a sense of fatigue. It is also to ensure that each part of the work receives sufficient attention.

Paganini: Violin Concerto No.1 in E flat, 3rd mov. bar 95.

One-movement versions of this work were published both by Kreisler and by Wilhelmj, perhaps partly to avoid having to play this passage of 31 bars of double harmonics. The work is nowadays played in D, a key which lacks the bite and sparkle of the original. Paganini tuned his strings up a semitone, a practice used by many viola players in Mozart's Sinfonia Concertante K364.

31

When working for technical accuracy
reduce intensity of expression,
but don't eliminate it—
work coolly, not coldly.

Ironing out a passage,
just seeking mechanical perfection,
can be counterproductive,
since later on you will need to begin again—
to work at the music.

Conversely, playing with full expression
before the technique is secure
can bring frustration,
particularly if the feeling is
that what was working yesterday
is not today.

ACCURACY

By temporarily reducing intensity of emotional output, attention can centre on the mastery of difficult passages. Control is increased by this kind of slow work. Time can then be spent on tone colours and widening the range of expression.

Playing with reduced expression can increase stamina when working in detail. It can also increase perspective on how much expressive energy is desirable in difficult passages.

Excesses of rubato or vibrato can then be more easily noticed. Too much use of expression can make a passage inexpressive, since it may lack variety. If your basic tone colours are too vivid, it can be hard to brighten them when highlighting certain passages.

Control of accentuation can increase clarity, both in grading the various written accents and stresses and in the exact expression of pulse within the bar. Playing with expression at a slow tempo can be another valuable stage in acquiring control.

Some ways of practising a semiquaver passage.

Those moments,
when the quality and balance of your work
reveal the presence of another dimension,
cannot be repeated.

They come in their own time
and cannot be found by grasping.

Don't expect them
or be disillusioned if they don't appear—
just seek balance
of control, expression and understanding.

INSPIRATION

Inspiration comes in its own time. When there is an unselfconscious balance between physical control, depth of expression and structural understanding, there may be moments in which another, deeper level in the music is felt.

The way forward is to seek balance in regular practice—not to wait around until feeling inspired. Self-evaluation should not be affected by the presence or absence of inspiration; the various states experienced are just part of growth.

Schubert: String Quintet, 1st mov. bar 58.

Inspired passages often have their own momentum—successful interpretation means not getting in the way of this.

Quality and regularity of work are essential—
let quantity be the amount of time
full attention can be maintained.
A good practice routine
keeps you fit, alert and absorbed.

Think before playing
and plan time carefully,
so that each moment is important—
the aim is to know what you are doing
and how and why you are doing it.

As well as tracing faults,
recognise things done well
and transfer them to memory for future use.
Then, by avoiding unnecessary repetition,
work will be creative.

ROUTINE

The question 'how long to practise?' is insignificant beside the question 'how to practise?'. Work calmly and with full attention and there will be much to discover. Spend time following up these discoveries and use them to good effect. There will be much to do, even on days when things don't come so easily.

The strength of purpose that makes us practise regularly can also help the organisation of a general plan of study. The morning walk, technical study and score study will then become natural parts of the day that we would not want to miss.

In learning technique and interpretation, we need constant awareness and understanding of what we are doing. Self-confidence and positive growth come from recognising achievements as well as faults. By observing which passages are played well, there is more time for those that need improvement.

Some aspects of musicality cannot be measured. When work is well-organised, it is more possible to materialise the imagination. The challenge for a musician is to develop a strong conception of a piece and then train the fingers to express it.

Mozart: Clarinet Quintet, 1st mov. bar 42.

Contrast this passage with the last example (p.35)—a personal touch is needed here in the shaping of this seven bar melody.

Think ten times and play once.

FRANZ LISZT

Don't just play the notes—make music!

PABLO CASALS

Conductors should have the score in their head, not their head in the score.

HANS von BULOW

PART TWO

HOMEWORK

Your natural musicality needs development and expansion.

Music is an art of infinite subtlety—it requires intuitive understanding and fine judgment.

To develop judgment you must know both how to look at a work and where to seek those passages and key moments that reveal its secrets.

Sing a phrase;
study the shape of the musical line,
to seek its contours of intensity.

Play it on your instrument,
making the fingers search for an ideal expression,
letting go of habits of technique that bring distortion.

Know the character and beauty of your instrument—
qualities that can enhance the phrase you have planned.

Feel a deeper value in virtuosity
realigned to express nuance and colour.

PHRASING

A clear idea of what you want to say will help to concentrate attention on the way phrases are shaped. Listen carefully and continu-
ously—often intentions are right but very little comes across.

Plan the dynamic contours of the phrase—certain notes will need
more emphasis than others. Decide where the phrase is going, which
are the high points and how much drive towards and through them
is desirable. Drive is containment and release of the energy of the
emotions—it creates movement through these high points, giving
direction and vitality.

Establish a clear sense of direction without hurrying—avoid the
pitfall of arriving at the point of maximum intensity one note too
early. Be sure to express the phrase as you have planned.

Consider its character—the beginning may need a specially chosen
colour and articulation, the ending a slight reduction in volume and
tonal intensity. The next phrase can then begin with clear articulation. Where there is fragmentation, or rests, keep an ongoing feeling
of musical line. Decide where to join and when to separate. Phrase
off wherever necessary—this is a must in legato playing.

Reduce the sound gradually, almost reluctantly, after the high
point of a phrase except when otherwise marked. Hang on to the
sound—don't let go of it too suddenly. (Tenors often do this well—
listen to them.) Be aware of the need for small diminuendos on resolutions, some cadences and on phrase endings. (Reduce the intensity
of the vibrato as you make these resolutions.)

Brahms: Piano Concerto No.1, 1st mov. bar 157.

Very clear contours, but this passage needs a contained energy and
emotion to reveal its reflective depth. Avoid impetuosity, particularly
by not hurrying the second half of bar 157, which must reflect the
nobility of the right-hand melody.

A piece of music is like the span of an arch.
It is a structure in which each phrase relates
to the one on either side,
as does each block of stone in the arch.

First consider the work as a whole,
then look at the various themes and sections
and individual phrases.

Enhance the beauty of each phrase
by letting it find its place
in the span of the whole work.

LINE

Examine the way phrases relate to each other. Some are joined, some need a clear separation, while others need just a breath between them. Take breaths where necessary within phrases—breathing is the natural guide to phrasing (see p.23).

Base the planning of phrase shapes on a clear knowledge of their length. Mark the ends of phrases in your score. The standard length is 4 bars: sometimes they are extended to 5, 6 or 7 bars, on occasion reduced to 3 or (rarely) 2 bars.

When the end of a phrase is not immediately clear, move forward to the next obvious ending. Count the number of bars from the last division, then consider different ways of marking the intervening phrases, until one way feels right.

Mozart: Symphony No.36, 1st mov. bar 20, 1st vln part.

Phrase lengths: 4 bars, 6 bars (3+2+1), 7 bars (3+3+1), 5 bars (3+1+1). Observation of phrase lengths shows cycles of activity. The most usual is: beginning, continuation, culmination, ending. Each part of the cycle needs an appropriate amount of energy to show its place. See this in the 4 phrases of the whole group (22 bars). This group is, in turn, the first part of a larger group.

This process can be expanded to embrace the structure of a whole movement. (Remember that both small and large groups vary in size, the same way as phrase lengths.) In sonata form, exposition, development, recapitulation are the largest divisions, the next in size will be the 1st and 2nd subject groups. (See p.55.)

When studying a solo
look at and play the bass line:

when studying a bass line
play or sing the melody.

Look at the harmony and rhythm of the inner parts
and experience the work as a whole.

An instrumental part has fewer page turns
but the score gives greater perspective.

INFORMATION

Keep the score by you for information and to consider each nuance in context. A separate instrumental part is useful mainly because it has fewer page turns. For serious study, instrumentalists should never be without the piano score. If your pianist needs a copy, buy or borrow another—this may seem inconvenient but there is no alternative.

In chamber groups, use a pocket score to learn how to integrate your part with the other instruments; also for such matters as phrasing, articulation and balance. Let the pocket score be standard issue for each player. You can also see your part in perspective in orchestral works.

From the score consider:

   —markings of breathing or phrasing from a wider perspective,
   —relative importance of themes in contrapuntal passages,
   —parallel passages in which the parts are interchanged,
   —fragments of melody passing between the parts,
   —tone colour in relation to the other instruments,
   —where a bass line is prominent, or a top line secondary,
   —the context of syncopated passages,
   —rhythm and note lengths in the context of the accompaniment,
   —tempo relationships from a wider viewpoint,
   —harmonic structure.

For concertos use an orchestral as well as a piano score. See how the planning of sound projection must relate to the instrumentation and resonance of the accompaniment. Note where to integrate with the orchestra.

Dvorak: Cello Concerto Op.104, 3rd mov. bar 477.

Observe how the 1st movement's restless motif, reawakened by the clarinets, is brought to a peaceful conclusion by the 3rd horn. This needs rhythmic continuity from the soloist after the trills.

An example of how interpretation can clarify structure (see also mus. exx. pp.21 & 97.)

When a world of expression
is contained in a few notes of melody,
it is the spontaneous approach
to what has been carefully planned
that makes it sound right.

Planning involves consideration
of the intensity of each note,
both in relation to its neighbours
and through its duration.
It also means discovering
a timing that makes it feel right,
an articulation that conveys character
and irresistible shadings of tone colour.

Spontaneity gives freedom
to follow the flow of intuition.

MELODY

Timing, rubato and tone colour are major elements in making a melody sound memorable. Also, finding the right mood and, where appropriate, cultivating a singing, legato style. When all these elements have been considered, forget them and just play from the heart.

To find the character and natural speed of a melody:

—look at its accompaniment, in particular the bass line,
—decide if the pulse is one or two in a bar (see p.53),
—look for any dance style—learn its inflections,
—look at the chord structure and speed of harmonic change.

See the melody within the context of the whole movement, and the contrast between the different themes:

—decide where it is going,
—where it ends,
—how to approach and leave its high points.

When the first note of a melody is an upbeat it usually needs a firm sound and articulation. Think of the upbeat rather than the following downbeat—this is the way to begin almost any such passage positively. After careful planning of a melody, play spontaneously. There is usually a melody or a passage that reveals the natural speed of a movement—experiment until it feels right.

Beethoven: Symphony No.2, 2nd mov. bar 82.
The dance character here reveals the natural speed of the movement.

Beethoven: Symphony No.9, 4th mov. bar 92.
A melody that moves in small steps finds its individuality in the larger interval—here in bar 103 the dynamics want it to be slightly stressed.

47

Rubato is giving as well as 'robbing'—
taking time needs to be balanced by moving forward.

Frequently, rubato in a melody
requires the background of a regular beat—
if both are displaced
the expressive aim may be frustrated.

In some works
rubato may stretch through several beats
or even several bars.
If phrasing is logical,
intentions will be clear
when moving on or taking time.

RUBATO

Rubato needs a sense of logic—it should not be mannered or repetitive. Don't be impetuous when moving forward or overindulgent when taking time. Beware of exaggeration in works performed frequently.

Style is the starting point when studying rubato. One type is used in baroque, classical and some 19th-century music. In the Franck Violin Sonata, 4th mov. any bending of the tempo is around a steady beat.

Here the rubato, in some bars, may slightly delay the 2nd, 3rd and 4th beats. Sometimes, in other works, the opposite is desirable—these beats can be brought forward, giving breadth to the end of the bar. To be effective, this bending of the rhythm should sound completely natural.

19th-century music sometimes needs a more complex rubato that stretches over several bars. Be aware of how much you are stretching the rhythm in both directions.

Brahms: Cello Sonata in E minor—2nd mov.—Trio.
The rubato can span the 4 bar phrase.

When playing in a group:

—don't slow up the music in a desire to be expressive,
—be precise on entry notes,
—agree on rubato when a melody moves between parts,
—make any rubato move around the beat in solo passages, unless agreed otherwise.

Consider, when learning a concerto or instrumental solo:

—which passages can be freely expressed with rubato,
—where you need to integrate (see mus. exx. on pp.45 & 97),
—where you must accompany.

Work at expression
can distort the sense of timing:
restoration of the rhythm
can feel like waking from a dream—
it is important to dream,
but also to wake up.

Rhythmic accuracy helps ensemble and texture.
Work at it before rubato,
checking length of notes, rests and ties,
especially in works often played.

Consider the speed of each section—
see that tempo changes occur
only at moments of expansion or moving forward.
Control of tempo
helps in making contrasts
of rhythmic character and style.

RHYTHM

Exactness and evenness of rhythm in itself brings music to life. The feeling of inevitability maintains the listener's involvement:

—where rubato stretches over several bars,
—in the stretched rhythms of certain dramatic climaxes,
—where a ritardando precedes a change of tempo.

Music for dancing has a beat that is regular and even. It needs an alive physical quality—so learn the steps. When a dance rhythm has the right emphasis, it is much more effective. Check contrasts of articulation and expression between passages. After slow practice, check for rhythmic steadiness. A metronome is useful at these moments—see if you are exact in moving off ties and if note values are observed.

When taking over a rapidly moving figure from another instrument:

—allow for the instrument's response time in the register used,
—allow for your own reaction time,
—sing in your mind the other part just before taking over.

Remember that repeated notes are rarely equal. When playing accompanying figures, slightly lighten each second note, or the second and third in a triplet rhythm. This is pulse in microcosm, and just as important (see p.52).

Mozart: Oboe Quartet, 3rd mov. bar 92.

An unusual moment in 18th-century music—the oboe part unilaterally changes to common time. If the cellist maintains a steady rhythm, all can proceed smoothly. Self-confidence is a major factor in rhythmic control.

The pulse is the rhythmic background to music,
uniting brilliance and drama
with the inner world of feelings and vision.
Choose this background with great care—
the relative emphasis of beats in the bar
that best expresses character and content.

Four beats in a bar are not equal—
usually third beats need less stress than first,
though more than second and fourth.
It takes much thought and experiment
to get these differences right.
If the beats are too similar
the playing sounds heavy.
The opposite occurs when accented beats are fewer—
it can seem lightweight
and the last beat of each bar
easily becomes hurried.

Focus on that vital distinction—
whether the feeling is one or two in a bar;
see if it changes with each theme,
or if changes in texture or accompaniment
are bringing other subtle influences.

This basic rhythmic plan
is often the foundation for a melody
that rises and falls independently.

PULSE

In a 4/4 bar, the 4 beats will not be of equal intensity. There is usually an underlying feeling of one in a bar, or two in a bar.

Consider the pulse in these passages:

1—Mozart: Piano Concerto K453, 1st mov.—one in a bar.

2—Bach: Oboe and Violin Concerto, 1st mov.—two in a bar. When the pulse is two in a bar, the second pulse will be slightly lighter than the first. The deciding principle is whether the music sounds heavy or lightweight—experiment until it seems right.

3—Mozart: Symphony No.40, 1st mov. This would sound lightweight in one, heavy in two. The solution is a light pulse on the half bar—somewhat lighter than the first pulse. Compare this with the slightly firmer second pulse of the Bach Concerto above. Consider the relationship between stronger and weaker beats.

In 3/4 time the pulse will be one in a bar.

4—Beethoven: String Quartet Op.18 No.1, 1st mov. When 2nd and 3rd beats are light, the music may have a bright, outgoing feeling. (Note the lighter pulse here on each 2nd bar.)

5—Brahms: Violin Concerto, 1st mov. When the beats are more equal, there may be a broader, reflective feeling.

Music has allure
and a life of its own
when the pulse between bars
is carefully graded.

The melody goes freely in its own direction,
while beneath it the pulse
regulates the flow
with its own pattern.

The two are independent,
yet united in their formation of the phrase—
there is no conflict
because the pulse is expressed by emphasis,
which is independent of dynamics.

METRE

Music is not a series of equal bars. Bars relate via the strength of their 1st pulse: very often in 4 bar groups. There is often variance between the shape of the melody and the pulse pattern:

— the melodic shape might expand to the 3rd bar and contract to the 4th.
— another phrase might be expanding through 4 bars.

In the standard pattern, the 3rd bar pulse is lighter than the 1st, but more than the 2nd and 4th. The domain of the pulse pattern does not stop at 4 bars (see p. 43).

Brahms: Symphony No.2, 1st mov. bar 82.

Here, the 1st beat of the 5th bar is clearly lighter than that of the 1st bar. As with phrase lengths, the size of the larger groups vary (here 20 bars—4×4+4 bars extension).

Beethoven: Symphony No.3, 1st mov. bar 1.

This is a 14 bar phrase (6+4+4. Here the first 2 bars are the extension). These groups are, in turn, part of a bigger group. In this way, there is a gradual merging of pulse pattern and overall phrase structure. The guiding principle is that while the shape of the melodic phrase structure is free-ranging, the pulse follows a more standard pattern. It can change for different sections of a piece.

Feel the movement of harmony
as the driving force
determining the speed at which music unfolds.

The movement away from
and back to the root position tonic chord
involves an increase and relaxation of tension
that provides essential support for a melody.
Study this in eighteenth-century music,
where drama and emotion
are expressed through relatively simple harmonies.

Bring this awareness into your playing:
feel the relative tension
of chords on different degrees of the scale
and the character of each harmonic progression.

Try this when accompanying—
differences in the intensity of chords
are often minimal,
but bring a new dimension of expression
that considerably increases dramatic impact.

HARMONY

Music is propelled by the movement of harmony as well as rhythm. Be aware of it in every piece you play—a basic understanding of harmonic progressions helps in finding the true pacing of music. Study this in Haydn and Mozart—observe the natural increase and decrease of tension when moving away from and back to the root position tonic chord.

Develop a sense of the weight and intensity required for each chord. For example, the progression IV, V, I. Feel how the strength of IV (whether subdominant or supertonic 7th, 1st inversion) is followed by a release of intensity from V to I. (The exception is where the return to the tonic is declamatory.) All music that has a tonic has this sense of departure and return. It is seen in the increasing harmonic ambiguity of 19th-century music, also in the atmospheric use of harmony and the percussive note clusters of the early 20th-century. The principle still applies, however tenuous the relationship is to the tonic. The pacing of harmonic movement may have nothing to do with the speed of the notes. After slowly moving harmonies, a swifter progression can create a sense of drama prior to a feeling of homecoming—or else a further plunge into the unexpected.

Consider the nature of melody notes that are not part of the harmony, especially when they fall on natural stresses. See if they are accented passing notes, or if they can be seen as creating more complex chords. Suspensions, with their tension and release, can act as springs that withhold and create motion.

Mozart: Symphony No.38, 1st mov. bar 241.

An interrupted cadence can need an increase of intensity from V to VI, (here via a chromatic passing chord).

Bach: St. Matthew Passion, No.54, bar 27.

The sudden appearance of a harmonically distant chord needs extra intensity.

Consider how notes begin and end
and how long they last.
There are many types of articulation
and different strengths of attack,
not just hard or soft beginnings.

Accents can be explosively brilliant,
biting, as they highlight the rhythm,
or even gently emphatic—
all are followed by a diminuendo,
which throws the accent into relief
and clarifies texture between the parts.

Notes with dots over them
can have many different lengths,
from very short to gently detached.
Dots within a slur
often need interpreting as lines.

Lines give individual emphasis
to notes in a legato passage
but can also mean a slight separation of the notes.

Slurs can refer to legato, phrasing or bowing—
when they show the linking of notes in a figure
the last note may need to be phrased off.

ARTICULATION

A printed edition can only be a rough guide to a composer's intentions. There are many ways to accent a note or interpret a line above a note. Consider the style—use trial and error to find what works best. There are two basic types of accent—one is percussive (ta), the other is more gentle (schrum).

Saint-Saens: Cello Concerto No.1, bar 1.
This is percussive.

Schumann: Cello Concerto bar 311.
This is more gentle.

Strong accents may be marked sf (sforzando means forcing). At the other extreme, Schubert's accents are often gentle inflections in the melody (see mus. ex. p.35).

On stringed, wind and brass instruments, make a diminuendo on a note that starts with an accent—on the piano this happens naturally. Accents on syncopations are biting, but only enough to show the cross-rhythm: they are followed by a sharp diminuendo.

A dot above a note usually reduces its length by half. In practice, notes with dots vary from being very short to 'dots plus lines'. Dots within a slur should be interpreted as lines (but this is not always the case in French music). A vertical line on the first of a group of notes with dots implies a slight kick on the note—to give impetus to the group.

A line above a note indicates a slight stress—but less than an accent. After the stress, separate the note very slightly from the next. Apart from this slight separation, hold the note for its full value. A note with a line never has a sharp beginning.

Develop exercises for the various types of articulations: e.g. for staccato, move gradually from smooth separate notes to very short ones and then back to smooth ones—do this at different speeds.

Dynamics are not fixed levels,
but a guide to the general level of volume
within which a phrase rises and falls.

Pianissimo needs a transparent quality
and conscious motivation
to reduce the level of sound.
Piano can require weight of tone—
quality of sound not quantity.
It can mean one thing in a solo,
another in an accompaniment.
Mezzo forte, being away from dynamic extremes,
needs added attention to tone colour.
Forte requires a full sound,
not necessarily of great volume,
but with depth and character of tone
and an unforced quality.
Fortissimo can then be noticeably louder—
with strength of tone
and a brilliant outgoing quality.

Plan crescendi,
so as to increase the level gradually.
Diminuendo is not a collapse of sound—
the direction of a melodic line
is usually better served
by gradual reduction in volume.

DYNAMICS

Develop a dynamic range that encompasses both sounds of great power and depth and also the lightest textures. Then there can be more flexibility when seeking the intentions behind dynamic indications. A marking is only an approximation of a composer's intentions: it refers to a general level of sound, but even this must vary in practice—e.g. playing a concerto in a large hall, or chamber music in a room.

Use dynamics with discretion in ensemble playing. Be continually aware of your part in relation to the others. Don't sacrifice tone quality in the search for dynamic contrast—there is a difference between a transparent sound and an insubstantial one. In loud passages, avoid hard strident sounds unless they are specifically indicated.

Beethoven rarely used mezzo forte, so forte and piano must cover a wide range of levels. In baroque and some classical music, dynamic indications are sparse. In 19th-century works, they create character and atmosphere. A crescendo has more effect when controlled. An example is the Rossini crescendo, which needs great patience in holding back the sound before the build-up to its climax. A diminuendo after the high point of a phrase should not deflate it—hold on to the sound, only letting go reluctantly.

Bach: Solo Violin Sonata No.1, 1st mov. bar 1.

This is intricate music, with a great range of content. Other than very few forte and piano sequences, there are no dynamic markings—they are left to the discretion of the performer, which is normal for the period. The manuscript is immaculate, and the carefully notated articulation can be a model for cellists, who lack such a source for the Cello Suites.

Do not play to be exact—it must be exact, but that alone is nothing.

NADIA BOULANGER

The speed of a runaway horse doesn't count.

NADIA BOULANGER

A semiquaver passage must be even, just as a dress must be well ironed—but not so much that, when your friend sees you, she exclaims 'Oh, how well ironed!'

NADIA BOULANGER

Part Three

REHEARSAL

Rehearsal is the art of doing maximum work with minimum friction. Before making comments, consider what you are doing and whether this is the cause of the problem. When making suggestions to another player, say what is not working and how it can be improved. Use a minimum of words, not long explanations—do this by knowing exactly what you mean. If you do not know, think about it; if still not clear, discuss it—but avoid slowing down rehearsals with long talks that are best held at other times.

Make suggestions about actions, but never criticise the person—don't speak impulsively. If you feel strongly about something, rephrase your first thoughts before speaking. Express your point in a way that is helpful and constructive.

By making a habit of consideration for colleagues, it is possible to put aside any artificial politeness. A rapport can then be developed which allows you to speak freely without inhibition. Avoid overloading partners with too many ideas at one time—just concentrate on points that are easily digested and remembered.

Each instrumental part is important.
Instead of solo and accompaniment,
think of different lines of music playing together.

Fragments of melody passing between instruments
need constant awareness of balance and texture;
when one part responds to another,
listening acquires another quality.

When players know the score,
parts providing harmony and rhythm
can produce moments of shading and colour
that may otherwise remain hidden;
yet however beautiful an inner part may be,
it must not be over-projected,
but find its place in the overall balance.

If playing as soloist,
the secret is knowing when to lead,
when to join with the other instruments
and when to follow them.

RESPONSE

A continual danger in ensembles is the competitive attitude. This can happen when each player is trying to outdo the other, whether by playing louder, more brilliantly or by over-zealous accompanying. A performance might end up as a struggle if the players are primarily concerned with projecting their own parts.

By contrast, the responsive attitude gives importance to the total sound. Each part is seen as a component of the whole: each player functions as a member of the group. At times, there is a need to be prominent, at others more in the background—respond at all times to the needs of the music and the other players.

Schubert: String Quintet, 2nd mov. bar 1.

The slow melody of the inner parts should not be upstaged by the comments of the 1st violin and cello.

The corresponding requirement, in a work for one or two players, is a feeling for the texture of the music and the relative importance of the different voices. Accompanying is the art of supporting, balancing and interacting with another player. Consider accompanying as important as playing a duo work. If the notes are relatively simple, you can give more attention to style, character, ensemble and rhythmic inflexion. In passages with rubato, decide where the accompaniment should follow, and where it must maintain a steady beat, around which the melody can revolve.

Ensemble can always be improved
but don't be obsessive,
or the playing will become clinical.

Stretch capacity in two directions—
play together to the highest standard,
and make music freely.

In a group many elements have to be matched
but, above all, let there be a wish to play together
and a balance between team work and individuality.

ENSEMBLE

Start with careful preparation—study the score and look at the notes before the first rehearsal. Detailed attention brings quality of ensemble. Be alert to rhythm and articulation, particularly when coming off ties, at ends of phrases with a ritardando and when the speed changes. In the group, agree a clear plan of interpretation. Be aware of structure when deciding details of ensemble. To play together, think and feel as a group.

In a string quartet (or any other ensemble), breathe together. Agree about types of articulation, character of vibrato and styles of bowing. Second violinists—cultivate strength of tone and rhythmic vitality and know when to lead. Violas—join them in being the rhythmic powerhouse of the group (or orchestra). First violinists—allow this—the top line will still be audible. Cellists—grade intensity of notes in relation to the harmony (see p.57).

Double bass players—be constantly alert to keeping up with the beat; this involves always allowing time for the instrument to sound. One way of working with this is to beat the cellist to the bow change.

Windplayers—coordinate breathing points, articulation, intonation and vibrato and match tone quality.

Pianists in ensembles—work at texture of sound, where to lighten the middle register (particularly in chordal or elaborate passages) and notes in the same octave as the instrumentalist. Transparency of texture is essential in a piano trio—avoid excessive volume by using energy without force.

Soloists—be sure that first notes of entries are not late.

Beethoven: String Quartet Op.18 No.6, 3rd mov. bar 1.

Not easy.

Concentrate on the note you are playing,
but be aware of what lies ahead.
Anticipate changes of speed or mood,
and the connection or separation of phrases.

Practise reading at sight,
keeping the eyes a bar or half-bar ahead,
according to the speed of the piece.
This brings a wider perspective
in timing, articulation and in relating phrases.

Practise also slowly,
caring for the whole length of each note.
See where notes are joined seamlessly
and where they need fresh articulation.
This brings a sense of timing
that is never hurried—
even in the fastest passages.

TIMING

Good timing comes from breathing with each phrase. It is a pacing of phrases that allows the music to unfold naturally. View the work as a whole to gauge changes of tempo, ritardandi and length of pauses.

Timing in ensemble needs awareness of rhythm and the response of your instrument in each register. A double bass or a tuba speaks more slowly than a violin or a trumpet. The response of a cello or an oboe is slightly slower in its lowest register than in its middle or upper ones.

Self-confidence allows rhythmic commitment with clear sound and articulation, especially at the start of a new melody or figuration. (Players lacking confidence often play slightly behind the beat, only feeling safe when someone else leads the way. By contrast, over-confidence can lead to playing slightly ahead of the beat.)

Practice of sight-reading helps the sense of timing. Make the eyes keep ahead of the fingers—don't allow the eyes to remain stuck on the bar that is being played. This widens the perspective, enabling anticipation of tempo changes etc. Conversely, when working in detail, care for a note throughout its length. Don't just have a momentary awareness of its beginning and then let the mind jump ahead. Give attention to unaccented notes, particularly the last notes of a group or bar. See that they are not hurried—let each note find its place within the phrase. When spending much time on detailed study, do a few minutes sight-reading to practise looking ahead.

When playing for many hours in an orchestra, or doing lots of sight reading, spend some time on slow notes, giving attention throughout their duration.

Make these techniques second nature—both are needed in performance. Attention to the beginnings of notes brings life to playing: extending it through the duration and endings of notes gives it breadth and beauty.

Strauss: Don Quixote, Var.3, 5 bars after 29.

With insistence and careful timing, Sancho Panza silences Don Quixote's interruptions, so as to air his complaints.

Seek quality of tone,
with depth as well as brilliance;
both are possible on a well-adjusted instrument.
Beauty of sound is important
but, if it becomes a preoccupation,
it limits the range of expression.

Letting loose the musical imagination
brings deeper understanding
of what the music is saying.
Each shade of emotion
then offers a fresh challenge
in discovering new colours.
Sound needs character,
with myriad types of intensity, inflection and texture.

TONE

Tone quality is a major part of expression, creating a response in the listener as it communicates varying colours and textures of sound. In part it comes from knowledge and experience on the instrument, but it also becomes the individual voice of the player. Whether singing or speaking it conveys emotion and dynamic intensity.

Good technique means being able to produce quality of sound at all dynamic levels and with any style of articulation. Beauty of tone is of great importance, but it is not a substitute for variety of sound. Each phrase needs its own character and colour—this is not easy if the basic tone is over-rich and highly charged. However, poor sound production can be unsatisfying even when it is varied.

The fundamental of a note is the lowest vibration of its harmonic series. When it is clearly present, tone has depth, presence and carrying power. On stringed instruments it comes from the correct ratio of arm weight and bow speed. On wind instruments it comes from diaphragm control.

The harmonic series on a low G.

Seeking depth of sound need not preclude brilliance—both are possible. It is not a case of having one or the other—your ideal sound can include both.

Vibrato is a device that is used to colour tone. Use it evenly, so that the individual oscillations are only minimally heard. Learn to vary it in speed and intensity.

Stringplayers—vibrato is most effective with good bowing, so practise sometimes without vibrato:

—to check the quality of sound produced by bowing,
—to check exactness of intonation,
—so that it is used for specific tone colours, not automatically.

Guitarists—practise sometimes with vibrato, which prolongs a note.
The parallel for pianists is to practise without pedal. This improves the accuracy of fingerwork. It also allows the pedal to be used to enhance or change colour and texture.

Never take intonation for granted—
the exact pitching of a note
is part of its expressive quality,
and each interval in the scale
has a different character.

Harmony is the best guide to intonation—
think of where a note lies in the scale
and its position in the chord.

The brightness
of slightly raised major thirds and sevenths
and the sombre quality of low minor thirds
show how the pitching of intervals
is an important element
when searching for the right tone colour.

INTONATION

Intonation is a way to find a closer contact with the harmony. In itself it is an expressive device that can create colour. Often its sensitive use brings greater depth to a phrase.

Train the ear to hear the exact pitch of intervals. Good intonation comes through constant alertness and correction.

Perfect and tempered intonation are used by instrumentalist and singers in different ways. In an ensemble, decide together which type of intonation is to be used. If a compromise has to be made, then this must be agreed.

Intonation can be used expressively. In a romantic instrumental work, a passage can be more effective when certain semitones are made smaller.

When playing in a group, a passage in a slow movement may need a chord to be tuned vertically, without reference to those on either side of it.

Ways of improving awareness of intonation in a group:

—tune the first chord of a movement slowly until it rings true,
—if in doubt, build it up from the bass,
—move to the second chord in a similar way,
—continue this process slowly through the succeeding bars.

Even if only a small section is rehearsed in this way, the quality of listening will be enhanced.

Beethoven: String Quartet Op.18 No.6, 1st mov. bar 70.
Agree as a group how to tune the C flat (bar 72).

See the formation of technique
as the development of physical movements
directed by the mind.

Understand each movement;
work till it is comfortable and in control.
Stretch your capacity in that direction
by inventing exercises—
different rhythms, articulations and speeds.

Command of physical movements
helps in moulding the shape of phrases.
Technique is a bridge
between instrumental facility and musicality—
the response of the hands
to each requirement of the musical imagination.

TECHNIQUE

There is a difference between technical control and facility—which is the ability to move fluently around the instrument. Technical control implies:

—quality and evenness of tone,
—control of notes throughout their duration,
—rhythmic exactness in difficult passages,
—absence of extraneous noises,
—exact articulation and intonation.

Technique is the shaping of notes to fit the phrase. Learn how to produce different effects on the instrument. It means an awareness of every sound and movement. Listen carefully while coordinating movements to form a phrase—it is not easy to notice errors that have been repeated several times. Hearing them is the first step to correcting them.

When a passage is not clear, examine the movements made and their timing. When necessary, make up exercises to increase control. Base these exercises on a particular movement—using different note patterns, rhythms, articulations and speeds.

Good technique means ease and absence of struggle. It means timing, clarity and tone quality. It implies possessing the means to shape the musical line.

Vieuxtemps: Violin Concerto No.4 in D min.1st mov. bar 80.

Great composers usually have more interest in music than in instruments. Composers who are virtuosi write music that lies well under the fingers—learning such works increases instrumental control.

Slow practice has a new significance
when bringing the threads of a work together.
It is finding clarity
to plan and put into order
those elements that become apparent
after resolving basic technical problems.

Detailed work embraces both content and style.
It is directing and controlling energy
to let phrases come alive,
and bring together all sections
through greater realisation of content.

DETAIL

There are two types of slow practice. One is playing at a reduced speed to increase control; the other is slow work at phrasing, balance of parts, harmonic direction, rubato etc. This allows work on the many details that may be missed when playing in tempo. It brings savings of time and energy, though at first it may appear to be a slow process.

Learning many pieces quickly can have the effect of limiting our understanding of them. We may either find it hard to make further progress, or else think that we know them. Practise calmly, not racing from one piece to the next. Learning a piece thoroughly means it can be revised more quickly—also memory becomes more secure.

Tchaikovsky: Variations on a Rococo Theme bar 22.

Deceptively easy—this theme always needs careful attention to its style and articulation. The strange indication 'gliss' before the high A (bar 27) may have been an early suggestion by Fitzenhagen. This cellist later enraged Tchaikovsky by his rearrangement of the work (omitting Var.8). His was the only version known for about 100 years until the original was published.

Virtuosity is not speed;
it is the means to create fire
that illuminates music.

It uses speed,
but never so much as to lose control
or render rubato impossible.
Rapid notes are always clear
and when they have melodic content
are not treated as passagework.

Sometimes music is brilliant,
needing a strong, dynamic approach—
rhythmic, articulated and outgoing;
sometimes subtle,
with depth of expression
and an inner reflective quality;
often somewhere between the two.

VIRTUOSITY

Virtuosity cannot be defined as playing fast. To develop it you need a well-coordinated technique, fine tone quality produced in a natural manner, a sense of timing, empathy with the innate nature of a piece and the spontaneous ability to generate excitement.

Once beyond the first thrill of being able to play a difficult work, examine every movement you make for efficiency and balance. Make complex passages clear, consider all details and look into every corner of the piece. Each animated passage will need fresh energy—find its exact character by practising sections of a movement separately, not always in the same order.

Music can be distorted by overindulgence in speed and brilliance. The danger is that expression, character and colour can be lost. The slightly slower tempo, in which the fastest notes are clear, creates more effect. If every note is heard, a passage sounds faster than when it sounds blurred and out of control. This because the animation comes from rhythmic exactness. A useful guide is to avoid a faster tempo than one in which you can use rubato.

Similarly, excessively slow tempi can be self-indulgent. Overconcentration on expression can make the music lose direction. When phrases are overrefined they become a series of elegant miniatures—the overall thread of connection may be lost. In slow, expressive passages, maintain rhythmic impulse and the direction of the musical line.

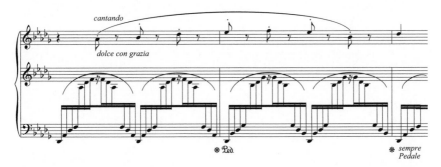

Liszt: Un Sospiro, bar 3.

When Liszt first heard Paganini play he became determined to emulate his virtuosity. In this Concert Study evenness of the melody notes, played by alternate hands, must be matched by smooth arpeggios.

Listen to yourself on a recording
to see if it sounds different
from what you hear while playing.

Note the differences;
use this information
to make listening more objective,
and to work at points not noticed before.

When performance and playback sound the same,
then listening has acquired a new dimension
and your work will have another quality.

OBJECTIVITY

In a recording studio, we have to listen to playbacks immediately after playing. This is fine for checking details, but it can be hard to gain a wider view of the performance. Try making a domestic recording before going to the studio. Then you will not have to sort out any changes to speed or interpretation during the session.

Wait until the next day before listening to the recording of a concert. By then your reactions will be more objective. Consider:

—technical accuracy,
—evenness of articulation or touch,
—the pulse (relation between stronger and weaker beats),
—the shape and continuity of phrases,
—contrasts of dynamics, articulation and tone colour,
—whether it sounds different from what was heard when playing,
—if the music flows naturally.

In early attempts at recording, don't worry if many things need to be improved. Focus on two or three areas—sort these out before proceeding to others.

Listen to yourself play as if hearing a recording. This involves an inner movement towards objectivity. Imagine you are a listener seated in the room, or a teacher or critic who has to comment on the performance. This way, begin to direct your own progress.

Brahms: Hungarian Dance No.1.

The composer announced: 'Ich bin Herr Doktor Johannes Brahms' at the beginning of his 1897 recording.

Listen through the duration of each note,
for fluency, variety and control.

It is too easy to close the ears
to that which we do not wish to hear—
doing this, even for a moment
encourages the habit.
Some faults are soon corrected;
others need careful analysis
to obtain the desired result.

Increased fluency frees the attention
and facilitates objective listening.
Then the way is clear
to find subtleties of phrasing and shading
that were desired but elusive.

LISTENING

Stringplayers should check:

—whether last notes of slurs are hurried,
—if bow changes are smooth and without noise or accent,
—whether the bowing is even and without bulges,
—if bowings used permit enough sound,
—if fingerings and bowings make the phrase smooth,
—if there is variety of tone colour and control of dynamics,
—if shifts are audible and any slides in good taste,
—if intonation is accurate and used expressively.

Woodwind players should check:

—for ease of tone production and quality on high notes,
—for evenness of tone across the registers,
—for precision of intonation,
—if articulation and fingerwork are coordinated,
—if entries are well-timed, particularly quiet ones,
—if the sound has sufficient dynamic control, flexibility of vibrato
    and tonal variety to blend with other instruments.

Brassplayers should check:

—whether intonation is controlled in each register,
—if the tonguing is appropriate for the articulation,
—if note endings are controlled,
—that the tone is full and rich, but without bulges,
—that the sound has enough colour and variety,
—that a real legato is being produced,
—if, on the trombone, the slide is being moved quickly enough.

Pianists should check:

—balance and synchronisation between and within the hands,
—if each note of a chord sounds as it should,
—if a note is prominent only by intention,
—if scale passages are even,
—for clarity and quality of sound,
—that a legato phrase is carefully graded,
—that the pedalling enhances the melodic and harmonic texture.

Beethoven: Symphony No.6, 3rd mov. bar 61.
    Listening to the approaching storm.

Tradition is the last bad performance.

IGOR STRAVINSKY

Why, in the twentieth century, do we play music of the eighteenth century in the style of the nineteenth?

NIKOLAUS HARNONCOURT

PART FOUR

BACKGROUND

A piece of music does not exist in isolation.

It is not a chance happening, but the product of a culture
and a composer's development.

Putting a piece of music on the stand
brings it into your world.
Balance this by entering into its world.

Consider a work
in the context of the composer's whole output,
and of many contemporaries—
painters, architects and writers.

Investigate this background
and those facets of personality
that reveal character and style.

Relate directly to the score,
but supplement this
with awareness of its historical context.

BACKGROUND

A piece of music often has a totally individual presence and atmosphere. With some pieces we find an instant empathy. If, with others, it takes longer, give them more time—it is a challenge, one that broadens the range of expression. Background investigation deepens the contact—there is always much to discover. Good performance is not just excellence of execution, but the understanding and reflection of a particular style and context.

The first step is to check the edition you are using. Note how it relates to the manuscript, first edition etc. Check what is the contribution of any editor. Do not accept it unquestioningly—another edition may be preferable.

Read about the life of the composer:

> —look up any available writings about the music,
> —find out about other works of the composer,
> —see if the work is part of a series,
> —learn about the style of the period from other works of art.

If, for example, you are studying a concerto by Beethoven, there is a journey of discovery to make. See how the nine symphonies compare with the seventeen string quartets, which contain many of his most intimate thoughts. Proceed through the piano trios, via the Triple Concerto to the violin and the piano concertos.

Expanding awareness and knowledge in this direction brings a further dimension of understanding.

Mozart: Clarinet Concerto in A, 1st mov. bar 187.

The modern A clarinet goes down to concert C sharp. Mozart's clarinet went down to A. This passage explores the richness of the instrument's lowest register. The modern clarinettist needs a special instrument, both for this work and the Quintet, to play all the notes (see mus. ex. p.37).

Each time you revise a piece,
remember the magic of the first time:
the score always yields fresh insights
to deepen understanding.

Knowing a work well
is to discover what you always knew was there—
a broader sense of timing
and an architectural view of the structure.

When first playing it in public,
attention is taken in many directions.
After this, preparation becomes more specific;
so much more is then possible
in refining interpretation
and consolidating technique.

EVOLUTION

Consider the preparation and first performance of a work as the first stage in learning it. Further study then brings greater detail and a deeper level of understanding. Keep a creative rather than a repetitive approach.

Listen to music of all types. Experience of a wide variety helps the understanding of works studied. They can also be considered from a larger viewpoint. You may then be more willing to experiment and take risks. Trial and error is part of growth—it can produce more dimensions to learning than can a safe and conventional route.

Listen to great performers. Compare recordings of a work to hear different approaches to its interpretation. In many historical recordings they seem to emanate from another set of values. Such recordings provide valuable information and are essential listening.

Devote some time each day to another art form. Discover great paintings, sculpture, architecture, literature, dance—all forms of art, both in man-made objects and in nature. Many parallels will become apparent—in the struggle and triumph of transcending limitations, the handling of form and structure and in personal expression of inspired visions.

Beethoven: Overture Leonore No.2 bar 392.

Beethoven: Overture Leonore No.3 bar 272.

The development of Beethoven's portrayal of the distant trumpet call representing the forces of freedom. In the final version, Fidelio, it was not included.

Style begins when we are prepared
to step beyond ready-made formulas
that superimpose an all-purpose musicality
on each work played.

Works of certain periods
may need different types of articulation
and tone production.
Certain emotions
are more appropriate to one age than another.

Choice of tempo of a movement
may be modified by historical research.
Every marking in a score should be observed.
If it does not agree with the conception,
the problem may be the conception
rather than the marking.

By considering all available information,
a feeling for style may begin to emerge.

STYLE

The 'spirit of an age' refers to those elements of human emotion and endeavour prominent at the time. Learning about this is the starting point for understanding a style. However, this does not mean that other emotions would be totally out of place. The fashions of the time would have seemed normal, so beware of eliminating all but a few carefully chosen elements. In the absence of a time machine there is no such thing as authenticity. This is because we are now operating in a different set of conditions.

Very often, succeeding styles are in direct contrast. Towards the end of a style's predominance, exaggerations might occur. The emergence of a new style may be partly in reaction to the excesses of the previous one. Each generation rejects or modifies the values of its elders. However overblown such proclamations of individuality may be, they at least help to maintain a sense of balance in the arts.

Nationality is another aspect of style. The music of different nations shows various permutations of emotions and values. Obvious examples are dances with a distinct ethnic, national or regional flavour. Generally, lighter music will show a higher degree of regional character. Consider colour, articulation and expression through the filter of nationality. Listen to great performers playing music of their own country. You may notice a natural approach performers from other countries lack.

Boismortier: Sonata Op.5 No.3, 4th mov. Menuetto.

Try 'inegal' quavers (unequal eighth notes) in bars 1,2,4,5&6; 'egal' (equal) quavers in bars 3&7, as they are not conjunct.

This is the French style of the period—the relative length of the notes was left to the discretion of the player. French music of the 18th century also used 'Scotch snaps' (also known as Lombardic), reversing the lilt of inegal (the short note comes first). Observe the parallel between this French style and jazz.

Examine the character of a work
to discover the range of emotions expressed—
sometimes they are conflicting,
sometimes complementary.

From a point of clarity
all these feelings can be projected.
Seek a response that is flexible—
one that moves swiftly between shades of expression.
Balance this mobility
with work at projecting depth of emotion.

To perform a work
it is not necessary to be in a particular mood—
just express its content.

EXPRESSION

To be expressive, first confront and examine any inhibitions and reticence. Daring to express a wider range of emotions is a fulfilling and rewarding experience.

Seek depth as well as variety of expression. Calming the breathing can slow down the mind. Then the emotional response joins with the direction of the thoughts. This state is like speaking with a deeper voice—finding the fundamental. This brings depth to playing.

Genuine emotion has an impact on the listener, who can be drawn from polite attention to real involvement. A display of emotion is not necessary—rather a deep level of honesty in the portrayal of musical content. This is the way to achieve a sense of presence in performance. It draws the listener to each phrase and to every shade of feeling expressed. Some emotions may come more naturally than others—work at widening the range by playing many styles of music. Even specialists will find the experience helps the chosen repertoire.

Brahms: Violin Concerto, 2nd mov. bar 1.

Expression comes from the way the long musical line is shaped. The oboist should breathe as if playing one long note, so as to produce an even sound: the violinist (bar 32) must be meticulous in bow distribution, limiting and grading the vibrato.

Consider the dramatic content
implicit in much abstract music.
Moments of drama occur
when sudden changes
in dynamics, rhythm or harmony
break the continuity of controlled situations.

When linking music to words,
a composer reveals
how figuration and harmony
are used to express the unfolding drama.
While parallels can be drawn
to help understand abstract music,
the individuality of each work
limits this process—
often imagination is the only guide.

To project the content of imagination,
develop a sense of timing and proportion,
and a dramatic sense
that encompasses a large range of dynamics—
from a storm to a whisper.

DRAMA

Drama in music, as in life, comes from the unexpected. Dramatic moments have more impact when occurring in normal situations, to which we can relate. Great composers have a developed instinct— they know how to place these moments so as to make them more effective. Operas and songs show the ways a composer expresses dramatic effects. Use this information to detect similar expression implicit in instrumental works.

Drama can be conveyed by an unexpected chord or harmonic progression. It can be by the sudden interruption or prolongation of a rhythm. Another device is an abrupt change of dynamic, whether as a furious outburst or a whispered sense of foreboding.

The interpreter's task is to evaluate and understand the significance of these changes so as to perceive their elemental power. Then it is possible to anticipate and project the intensity and duration of these moments. Much depends on a sense of timing—how to place a chord, knowing where to stretch a passage or press on without lingering. A wide range of dynamics heightens such effects—steer between overeffusiveness and reticence.

Don't try to create drama where it does not exist, but allow freedom of expression where it does. By refining that free expression learn how to express drama in music.

Verdi: Requiem, No.7 bar 1.

Dramatic intensity is intensified here by intoning the words on one note.

Consider the inspiration of a work,
its structure and the feelings conveyed—
they are there to be discovered.

Do not limit yourself
by superimposing ideas—
go towards it with a clear mind
and listen to its deepest message
with the inner ear.

Relate to it from your innermost feelings,
embracing its expression
so that the work becomes your own.

DEPTH

When beginning the study of a great work, use observation rather than ideas. Observation can function on many different levels:

- —noting every marking in the score,
- —examining form, structure and harmony,
- —examining the shape of the melodic line,
- —understanding the phrase structure,
- —considering emotions and moods expressed,
- —discovering rhythmic structure and tempo relationships,
- —understanding any connections with other works.

Develop the ability to hear the work in the imagination: make each detail and nuance relate to the overall conception. The next stage is to decide how to interpret the music. This will involve decisions based on information gathered. Decisions may be about phrasing, rubato, articulation, expression, style, characterisation etc. Works of an overtly romantic nature, programme music and some lighter pieces will need a certain personal expression—but keep within the stylistic limits. Draw expression from the text, don't superimpose on it.

The essential step in achieving depth is to put structural integrity before personal expression. An example of this is the 1st movement of Beethoven's Violin Concerto. The symphonic nature of the writing often involves the violin taking an obligato role, so as to maintain the rhythmic flow. Play the upbeat triplet here in time, so as not to interrupt the drum beat motif, on which the whole movement is based.

This part of the development section is also based on the drum beat motif. Keep up the speed so as to make this clear—here it is played by the horns.

Don't play at home and practise in public.

JASCHA HEIFETZ

To give a hundred per cent, you must be two hundred per cent prepared.

JASCHA HEIFETZ

To be a soloist you need the nerve of a bullfighter, the concentration of a Tibetan monk, the digestion of a peasant and the vitality of a nightclub hostess.

JASCHA HEIFETZ

PART FIVE

PERFORMANCE

The art of performance has been described as 'forgetting what you have been taught'. Thinking for yourself and being suitably prepared gives the possibility of finding a spontaneous approach in public.

Whether you are playing to one person in a room, or to several thousand in a large hall, performing is radically different from practising. Project the music and make it intelligible to the audience. A sense of timing, a fluency of delivery that finds the natural flow of the music, and the ability to make the sound carry to the back of the hall, are important.

Timing can involve necessary adjustments of speed or delivery to suit the acoustics of a hall. Planning the sequence of events on stage is also important. A concert begins well when the performer walks on stage projecting a sense of confidence and openness to the audience.

An audience listens. If you have been listening carefully while practising, and can do the same while performing, then you can effectively invite the audience to listen with you. Such awareness of what you are doing will lead you to choose works that you can perform fluently. Physical control gives more space for refinement of interpretation.

Performing conditions rarely seem ideal. It may be too hot or cold, the piano, the chair or the acoustics of the hall may not be ideal, a string may be false or a reed may be giving trouble. If well prepared, you can usually take these things in your stride.

An audience loves to be entertained and will respond enthusiastically to a player with strong personal projection. However, there is a difference between an appealing performance which brings the house down and a satisfying one that seems to touch the very nature of the music. One may be forgotten by the next day, the other may remain in the memory.

Any kind of performing
is difference from practising:
it is the moment of truth
when quality of preparation is revealed.

Practise performing:
play to friends before concerts
as an essential part of preparation,
especially when playing works for the first time.

These occasions will help in many ways:
to see a work as a whole,
check speeds and tempo relationships,
test technical security,
project outwards and eliminate inhibitions
and to work off any surplus nervous energy.

Recording these sessions
gives added perspective.

PREPARATION

The transition from study to performance can provide a two-way input of information. In performance—awareness of deficiencies in preparation: in practising—anticipating problems in performance. This is a way to further develop practising technique.

A similar process can be applied to interpretation. Compare the recording of a concert to how it sounded at the time. This helps timing and the joining of sections to make a balanced whole.

In a concert, take note of how the instrument feels in the hands, of breathing and if you are physically comfortable. Note what causes concern and whether this is real or imagined. See what happens when the breathing is calmed, with focus on what is being done.

Mozart: Eine Kleine Nachtmusik, 1st mov. bar 1.

Think one in a bar, the pulse of each second bar slightly lighter, and the rhythm exact. Some pieces are easier than they sound—this one is the opposite, particularly as regards intonation, ensemble, pulse and general performance standard.

Playing a work from memory
means unfolding the broad lines of its structure
and detailed facets of its beauty
without external prompting.

To find security in performance
cultivate four types of memory:
aural, harmonic, tactile and visual.
If one memory for a moment is uncertain,
then another will ensure survival.

The score, in performance,
can be either a reference point for details,
(if it is known virtually from memory
and is being used just as a reminder),
or a barrier
between performer and audience.

MEMORY

To some performers, memory comes naturally—others have to work at it. As with anything else, it improves with practice. Leschititzky told his pupils that if they would memorise a page each day, they would have a whole trunkful of music by the end of the year.

Certain passages should receive special attention. For example, where a theme returns more than once but continues each time in a different direction—confusion can occur. Note the sequence of these passages, so as to make the memory secure: the same where any memory lapse occurs in playthroughs. This builds trust in memory.

The memory functions best when there is no awareness of it and concentration is on the music. However, development of different types of memory brings added security. Harmonic memory is the ideal backup to melodic memory, since it helps in maintaining the thread, even by improvising if necessary. It is not generally affected by any lack of self-confidence. If all else fails, tactile memory will carry you through. Visual memory helps in knowing where you are, especially in long movements.

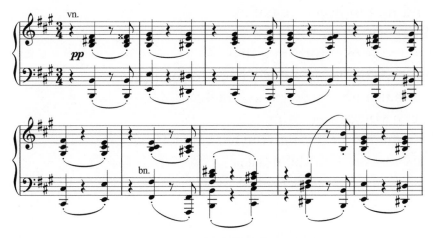

Schumann: Piano Concerto 3rd mov. bar 80.

This passage, which begins with the orchestra, is a major test of a pianist's memory. Plan a precise route map, knowing which turn to take at each junction.

Breathe slowly and deeply
when waiting to go on stage.
While walking on, consciously relax,
and open out the attention.
Feelings of nervousness
or overconfidence while playing
are equally undesirable—
curb them by breathing evenly,
concentrating on the phrase being played.
Overconfidence can cause a mistake
that disturbs the concentration.
Conversely, even when nervous,
the fingers always keep going,
and that in itself is calming.
Imagine the two states
as opposite points on a dial—
keep bringing the needle back to the centre
so that both states are avoided.
Then you can be calm,
eventually forgetting yourself altogether,
and at one with the music.

NERVES

Rapid constricted breathing is the biggest cause of nervous tension, before and during a performance. To feel calmer, breathe slowly and deeply, filling the lungs completely (see p.122). Good preparation brings a feeling of being on top of things. Preparation is not just practising, it is making ready in all ways to go out in front of an audience and perform.

Somewhere between a month and a day before a major performance, there may be a sudden awesome feeling as the realisation of what is coming strikes home. This is quite normal and soon passes; it has the positive aspect of preparing the nervous system for the occasion.

A positive step towards releasing surplus nervous energy is the giving of practice performances. What matters most is the feeling on the big day. Always time the journey to a hall so as to allow plenty of time for warming-up and for any unforeseen problems (most concerts have one or two). Avoid being in a hurry.

Mozart: Serenade for 13 wind instruments K361, 3rd mov. bar 1.
Sometimes the magic of a work can make us forget ourselves.

Pace yourself carefully on concert days—
rest well and avoid overrehearsing,
saving energy for the performance.
Project a feeling of enjoyment
and commitment to the music:
learn to maintain concentration
during any noise or movement in the hall.

In the early part of a concert
it is easy to imagine
a coldness on the part of the audience.
The need for the approval of others
before giving value to what is being played
may bring unsteady concentration
and inhibition of movements.

With trust in your own judgment
you will be pleased by a good reception,
but not devastated otherwise.
Don't try to please everybody—
that is weakening:
do the best possible
and believe in what you are doing.
The audience is not there to judge
but has come to be entertained:
enjoy the music
and everyone will enjoy it with you.

PACING

Consider the way you feel, just before going on stage, and in the early part of a concert. Compare this with the way you feel at the start of a concert you attend as a listener, and the apparent state of the people around you. This exercise shows how listeners want to be entertained and inspired—to experience what the player has to communicate.

Rather than getting caught in a vicious circle of subjective worries, be open to the audience and share what you have to say. An audience responds when a performer appears confident and secure: nervousness and tension can have the opposite effect on listeners.

Always maintain focus during a concert. Don't get concerned about any slips, or carried away if it goes well—both are self-conscious states.

Chopin: Polonaise in A flat, bar 33.

Certain works have a strong effect on audiences which, in turn, helps the performer. When played as an encore, the effect is heightened.

No matter how distinguished you become, there will always be fifty per cent of the audience who say 'Isn't he marvellous!' and the other fifty per cent who say 'Ah, but you should hear so-and-so, he's much better!'

CLAUDIO ARRAU

You must play in such a way that they have no choice but to engage you.

ROGER CHASE

Part Six

POST MORTEM

Concerts can be an accelerated learning experience. In performing to an audience we can assess the viability of our technique, expressive capacity and handling of a piece.

When things go well it can be exhilarating and enjoyable. Yet it can happen, especially in our early concerts, that all does not go as planned.

Any analysis of the performance should wait until the following day. Then things can be considered in a more detached manner.

It is unusual to be good at everything,
but easy to cultivate strengths,
while neglecting what does not come naturally.

Seek an environment
that will encourage growth in these areas,
and the confidence to persevere.

By creating a habit
of daily work at weaker points,
this feeling for balance
will later be of benefit in more subtle areas
and your playing will continue to grow.

PERSPECTIVE

Courage and resolution are needed to focus actively on weaker points. There may be great progress in certain areas, while in others there is not only less ability, but lack of self-confidence to come to grips with the problem. One way round this is to keep to repertoire that feels safe. The other is to confront the problem and form a habit of working at it every day. This may need patience if progress is slow, but such work will have a marked effect on all-round abilities.

Apart from specific focus on a problem, there is a need for more general awareness of what is helpful. A problem of technique may require a willingness to change fundamentals. At the same time it needs emphasis on physical exercise, good posture and breathing. In problems connected with expression, consider motivation and any emotional inhibitions. Review also techniques of expression.

Sometimes weaknesses are less obvious and are obscured by early success. An active schedule can help self-confidence and growth in weaker areas. Yet a problem might also become buried deeper through a need to compensate for weaknesses. Sooner or later, it must be examined—this is essential for further growth.

Brahms: Symphony No.1, 4th mov. bar 47 (trombone parts).
This is a test of the all-round ability of trombonists.

Many problems can be solved
by detailed consideration and analysis.
For some others, stand back
to gain a wider perspective
and adopt a commonsense approach.

Sometimes the difficulty faced
has a deeper origin:
the apparent problem may seem complex,
yet its underlying cause
can be more straightforward.

Trace effect back to cause
to reveal the nature of a problem:
a single discovery
may bring the key to the situation.

PROBLEMS

Problem solving is a part of creative thinking and a valuable skill to develop. Some problems are overcome by regular focussed work. However, there is a difference between problems that can be handled by a direct approach and those that reflect something deeper. Sometimes a direct approach only produces frustration. A wider awareness is necessary at such times.

Retrace the chain of cause and effect to discover an underlying problem. When the link between cause and effect is clear, the solution is often self-evident. Such work involves stepping back and examining the situation from different angles. An example of this is when a held muscle manifests as a physical tension in another part of the body.

Difficulty in mastering a certain passage can point to a specific fault or misunderstanding of basic technique. Tracing and eliminating this can bring benefits far beyond the mastery of that passage. In such a case, continued practice might not have solved the problem.

From the wider perspective, commonsense solutions can also be discovered. These may concern breathing, posture, regular exercise and avoidance of overwork. A willingness to consider new ideas may reveal the clinging to a half-understood idea that was never suitable.

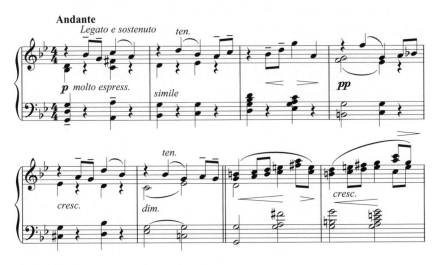

Elgar: Enigma Variations, bar 1.

The enigma is the identity of the well-known tune on which this theme is based.

The best source of self-confidence
is knowing what you are doing
and being in control of it.
Experience is another part—
it is easier to be confident
in works already performed.

In a concert,
focussing on an aspect of the music
or of the playing,
helps to develop an ability
to bypass random thoughts
that carry seeds of self-doubt.

Self-confidence brings a feeling of expansion
that gives a healthy ring to our playing
and increases powers of communication.
However, don't let it become exaggerated—
it is best to be immersed in the flow of music
and not interfere with the process.

SELF-CONFIDENCE

If self-confidence grows with abilities, it is less likely to be affected by criticism, or any temporary setbacks. Try to keep a clear and realistic view of progress made. Always be aware of the highest standards, especially if you are one of the best performers within a certain circle. This is the way to avoid the shock of having to adjust to the standards of the outside world.

There is a great difference between using the mind to plan technique or interpretation and the self-conscious procession of stray thoughts that sometimes circulates. These thoughts don't easily go away—handle them either by not giving them attention or by pausing to follow one through to its conclusion. Focus the mind in a positive direction of choice.

Avoid concentrating on the technique in a way that may interfere with its function. After training the fingers, learn to trust them in performance. Don't use the eyes to direct them. Rather, train the hands and arms to gauge distances unaided—enjoy moving around the instrument and taking risks. This makes possible a new level of accuracy.

Bihari: Rakoczy March.

This lively tune radiates self-confidence that is stimulating for both players and listeners.

Sometimes we run around chasing our tails,
and at other times are too lazy even to move—
between these two points there is a state of poise,
from which to speak clearly and act wisely
and find freedom in work.

Focus on mechanical technique
might create a division
that inhibits the natural flow of musicality.
Similarly, avoid being too emotional,
too intellectual,
or obsessed with inner meaning.
To progress further in one direction,
first create a balance.

Finding the cause of any block
will bring new energy and incentive.
It may mean being very honest
but is worth the effort.
In the act of balancing there can appear
a more realistic assessment of needs.

POISE

If there is a feeling of being blocked and unable to progress further, it may be caused by having overemphasised one aspect of the work. The solution may lie in turning to neglected areas.

If the head feels overused and dried up, try working at emotional and dramatic content.

If too emotional and unfocussed, devise a positive plan of action.

If earthbound through technical grind, put down the instrument and look at the score.

If the head is in the clouds, return to earth by working at technique.

There is another common cause of blocks—going in the wrong direction and being slow to realise it. In that case, put the instrument aside, think through the situation and then follow your instinct.

Blocks are often caused by an obsession with what should be done. Once this problem is recognised, it is easier to overcome.

Mozart: Horn Concerto No.3, 1st mov. bar 29.

Poise in a melody.

Constant observation and study develop perception;
learning to use perception brings insight.
View criticism constructively—
it can add dimensions to our work,
while compliments might dull sensitivity—
too much of anything
is as bad as too little
and as much of a distraction.

We are our own best teachers,
but only after learning how to study
and be attentive both to overall form and detail.
Until then we need someone
who will prepare us for this work
and then slip into the background
as the work becomes internalised.

By listening to others,
not accepting or rejecting but just listening,
we find the way that works:
by keeping open to ideas,
there is always something new to learn.
Self-confidence grows as we learn to discriminate
and to trust our own judgment.

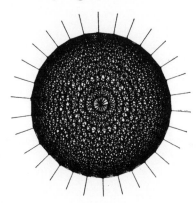

JUDGMENT

Make music come alive by trusting perception and observation. Advice, theories and ideas sometimes lead in the right direction, but in the end you must make your own decisions.

Theories are relevant if there is a direct, practical connection and they are seen in that context. If taking ideas from other performances or recordings, first see the reasoning behind them. Copying a point may be totally illogical in the context of your own interpretation.

The danger of too much advice is that there is not sufficient opportunity to make your own mistakes. Then your ideas can seem less viable than the convential view. (This is especially true when preparing for a major performance or competition—see p.121.) Give value to your ideas, but be selective. They should be thought through, not judged while in an embryonic state. Always the test is— do they flow naturally from the needs of the music, or do they super-impose upon it?

Haydn: String Quartet Op.76 No.5, 3rd mov. bar 1.
Wisdom in a melody.

FURTHER THOUGHTS

In a master class, Pablo Casals was asked how much he practised. The student replied, when invited to name his own time first, 'Seven hours a day'. Casals said that he had never practised more than four. He had always been out in the world, experiencing life, so that when he played he would have something to say.

CREATIVITY

Traditionally, performing musicians were also composers. Early in the 20th century the two roles began to divide.With the rapidly increasing prominence of recording, performers became ever more conscious of the need for excellence and reliability of execution. The training of musicians increasingly became based on learning instrumental technique at the expense of wider skills. The proliferation of international competitions had a further narrowing effect. Contestants often thought that they would be more successful if they followed safe, traditional patterns of interpretation. The negativity of such an approach can be countered by a reappraisal of creativity in music making.

If composing is a creative art, performing is a reproductive art, but one which needs a creative approach. Composing music, improvising, writing cadenzas for concertos, even arranging music will stimulate creativity. Any efforts in these directions, however modest, will add to our creative ability. By writing music we can better understand the minds of other composers.

If we can touch on the creative process we will want to bring it to our interpretations. Structural understanding of works we perform will become a priority, as will the grasp of harmonic implications and nuances of pulse. The search for style will lead to many parallel works for comparison. This does not involve so much the abandonment of performing traditions as their re-examination. Everything will be related to the information in the score and how we wish to express it. The act of realising a composer's intentions will then acquire a new and deeper significance.

BREATHING

Proper breathing is a fundamental part of playing and performing. Singers and windplayers depend on it for sound production; for players of keyboard, stringed, plucked and struck instruments, it is something to be learnt.

When breathing in, allow for the expansion of the rib cage, particularly in the back. On the out breath, these same structures release inwards like a set of bellows. This release prepares the body for the next breath. Good breathing is cyclical: after breathing out there is a moment of rest before the next inhalation.

Poor breathing often occurs by lifting and narrowing the chest. This interferes with the free movement of the arms. Tension in the muscles of the neck is a contributing cause to such breathing.

Free relaxed breathing is an essential part of good phrasing, both in avoiding tension in the body and in sensing the shape of phrases. Observe the breathing while practising, then note whether it changes when playing to somebody.

Remember, particularly before your first concerts, that the best antidote to pre-concert nerves is calm and even breathing (along with knowing your notes). Conductors, or leaders of a group, should breathe while giving the upbeat. If waiting for the upbeat, breathe with it when it comes. Speaking to an audience gives a further opportunity to watch and to free the breathing.

PLATFORM MANNER

It is not just the playing that matters, but also the way you present yourself and are received by the public. In any solo or chamber music concert, or if conducting any sort of group, entrance and exit are important parts of a performance.

At the end of the rehearsal before a concert, check the position of chairs, stands and anything else used. If the music is on the stand, see that it is correctly arranged and open at the first page.

Check the breathing before going on stage, then walk on confidently, however you are feeling, head up and looking at the audience. Put aside worries and concerns—the audience has come to hear you, so be there for them. In making a bow, whether brushing the hair against the floor or just giving a nod, come back as high as the point you started from. Continue to give attention to the audience for a moment—a bow must have an end as well as a beginning. When bowing, don't clasp the hands together in self-protection, or fling one hand in the air when coming up. If carrying music, only now should it be put on the stand.

If tuning the instrument on stage, leave a clear silence between the end of the tuning and the beginning of the piece. This is particularly relevant for guitarists, whose tuning is more melodic than open fifths or a single A. If you tune the instrument between movements, do it very quietly.

If any slips are made while playing, don't grin or look miserable. If there is any problem with memory, the best is to improvise via the harmonic memory till the thread is picked up (particularly in concertos). If playing alone, an alternative is to continue from a known point, in such a way that most people will not notice that anything has happened.

At the end of the piece, don't touch the music. Give attention fully to the audience. However well or otherwise you have played, acknowledge the applause as before, and only then pick up the music (if necessary), before leaving the stage. If you are recalled to the stage more than once and wish to play an encore, announce it loudly and clearly. Otherwise there will be a muted murmur of 'What was that piece?' Choose encores carefully for the occasion—don't emulate the pianist who chose Bach's Goldberg Variations.

THE SOLOIST

What qualities are needed to make a career as soloist? Consider the matter from the way we use our own judgment when comparing several recordings of a solo work. Some players offer a brilliant and accurate rendering but not much more. After eliminating recordings which don't manifest strong musical character, versions where the temperament doesn't seem to fit the piece are put aside. Amongst the remainder, perhaps only a few seem to portray the essence of the music in a way that we find really interesting. Don't follow the commercial trend by limiting the choice to soloists whose recordings currently line the shelves of high street shops. Make a deeper search to find out which are the finest since recording was invented.

To progress as a performer, it helps to become a discerning critic. Rather than idolize one player, assess the pros and cons of the main contenders. Look for a recording that has some special quality—feelings about this may well change from day to day, but generally we have a few favourites. Ultimately, if we have a contribution to make, the ideal performance will exist only in our inner ear or while reading the score.

*　　*　　*

Is it possible to aim towards the same standard of interpretation as that required by our objective judgment? Which is the route that leads in that direction? The ability to dazzle audiences with luscious tone and virtuosity in our early years may put us in demand. If things go well, offers can suddenly escalate. Providing that a sufficiently wide repertoire has been prepared, much can be learnt from public performance. Conversely, if too many offers are accepted, there is a danger that development can be impeded. Wise advice is needed about how best to balance the schedule of study and performance.

The thrill, when first acquiring facility and expressive ability, continues and grows with the gaining of strength. The early stages of a solo career may consist largely of concerto dates. This is ideal for the dynamic energies of a young virtuoso: such expression is of great importance. It is about developing strong personal projection that conveys a wide range of emotion. It is one thing to sound good on a recording, another to have a tone that sounds dynamic from the back of the hall—one that can captivate an audience.

*　　*　　*

When the time is ripe for the next stage, it can be at first confusing to realise how different it is. It must come at the right time, when secure in both technical and expressive abilities.

This is the time to ask yourself how far you want to go. Learning about deep musical values may not produce instant, tangible results, because maturity is not achieved overnight. However, there is the satisfaction of moving towards an ideal and, once on track, new abilities are soon developed.

When playing great music, technique becomes a search for the required expression. No longer just at the service of virtuosity, it acquires new dimensions. A Beethoven or Brahms Sonata or solo music by Bach requires a wide range of emotion, subtleties of phrasing and tone colour. To be played convincingly it needs an intellectual grasp, and the ability to reflect the broad line, the details of phrasing and of expression.

When learning this musical language, it becomes clear that the best contribution lies in complete fidelity to the score. It can be amazing to discover hidden depths that were previously unseen. This has a resonance that goes beyond the world of personality. A strong inner response to this is a normal part of development. See it in context as part of the whole picture (see p.96).

From this quieter point, it is more possible to sense the creativity of the composer. Understanding this process facilitates its expression in performance (see p.121). Mozart just heard music in his inner ear and wrote it down. Brahms, in the last year of his life, said that his method of composing was to diffuse his mind until he was receptive to music that came to him from the ether. Then he used his craft to give it form and substance. His lifelong friend, the great violinist Joachim, responded that at last he understood why Brahms was a first-rate composer and he only a third-rate one.

* * *

Awareness of the human dimensions of the composer's personality, as well as the drama of a descriptive piece, is a part of musical insight. Musicality is not just about depth, it is also finding and expressing the character of each work played.

Specific musical values, particularly as regards character, are not confined to the deepest works. Consider an example at the other extreme—Paganini's Violin Concerto No.1 (see p.31). Much work may have been done to make a clean and near-perfect version, but objective listeners want a version that also brings out the lyrical romantic quality and flows beautifully, rather than sounding like a compendium of tricks. The 4/4 first movement needs a carefully graded two in a bar pulse; in the 2/4 Finale a two in a bar pulse (always lighter on the second) grounds the movement so that it does not sound flippant. By adding to this an understanding of the metre i.e. the way the bars relate, the flow can be found.

Pulse and metre (pp.52–55) are generally the least understood aspects of music making. The danger for players who prefer instinct to analysis is that almost everyone is naturally better at some things than others—so there is usually a need to analyse aspects that give difficulty.

There is not just one way of playing a great work. From the recordings it is clear that, to be outstanding, a performer must also speak with an individual voice—in a way that is important to the listener. Individuality comes from development of the personality and from experience of life (see p.120). Remember that romantic works generally involve the personality of the performer more directly than do works of the classical period.

It also comes from experience of the wider world of music. A cellist, for example, working at the Solo Suites of Bach, should know intimately his solo works for violin (see p.61) and listen to the keyboard works and cantatas. Include also lieder recitals and operas (to learn about tone colour, emotion and drama in music), visits to great art galleries and cathedrals, reading Shakespeare, history and languages. It is not just how much is assimilated, but about being open to the whole world of culture. It is an alternative world to the manipulations of modern technology (which is invaluable in its own way)—each person decides how time is to be used and valued.

Discover the chamber music repertoire, both as player and listener. Performing chamber music is of enormous help to a soloist, to develop listening, timing, flexibility and for the contact with great music. If playing in a symphony concert, be aware of how different composers use the orchestra. Compare the way they create effects and use instrumental colour. Study the scores of symphonies—try learning the elements of conducting (see p.127). When everything is seen as a stage of development, any type of music-making is absorbing.

*   *   *

Career possibilities come through a combination of ability, hard work and good luck. Discover, through trusted advisors, what is lacking in your playing—before the critics do. It is better to know the truth in advance, while there is still time to put things right. In a competitive world, this can make all the difference. Don't try to be perfect, because this is limiting.

Certainly, for the young virtuoso, agents, recording contracts and major dates are important. However, if over-reliant on just talent and promotion, a soloist can be dropped as easily as taken up. Without continuing musical development, careers nowadays can be very short. There is room for only a handful of performers at the top level, and even those well-established face competition from new arrivals. The best preparation for a career is to carefully develop all aspects of playing. Be first a musician.

CONDUCTING

HOMEWORK
Conducting needs precision, but it is not a precise art. It cannot be measured, but must control a measured rhythm. In this sense it coordinates a group of players: from a larger viewpoint, it is an act of interpretation. Craft facilitates rehearsal—artistry and musicality create the performance.

The first step is to free the shoulders and arms, along with the breathing, so that no joint is inhibited. Know all beat patterns as second nature—learn to change instantly from one to another. The beat needs a natural bounce, with enough point to be clear, but not so much as to be clinical. The shape of the beat is determined by the music's character. It must be conveyed a moment before it happens—on the upbeat, not on the downbeat. No sympathetic movement of the head while beating—especially when shaping a phrase, making an accent or an emphasis.

Practising with records only helps when learning beat patterns. It is following rather than leading—the opposite of conducting. The major exception to this is when learning to follow soloists, especially in sections with rubato or many changes of speed.

Being in front of an orchestra is a direct experience—the degree of preparation determines what is learnt from it. Work out and mark all phrase lengths, be aware of each instrumental entry and its dynamic. Decide where a look is necessary and where to give a gesture—if the players don't know a work, more cues are needed.

From an intimate knowledge of the score, plan what you want before the first rehearsal. With the orchestra, be aware of all that is happening and ready to adjust your demands accordingly. Speak to the players in a clear and resonant voice, always using as few words as possible—never ten when two will do. Often a word while playing will save stopping. Be definite in your ideas, but always helpful and understanding. Play, whenever possible, whole sections of a work. Then go back for a few relevant points. There is an art in perceiving the key to a rehearsal problem—whether it is rhythmic, balance, dynamics, tuning, articulation or something else.

REHEARSAL
Your beat must be clear from all quarters—use a podium so that the players can see you. Focus attention frequently towards the back of a string section, to ensure their involvement and exact timing.

String sections always need encouragement and control of dynamics. They also need help with styles of bowing, types of vibrato and textures of sound. Sensitivity of articulation is important, e.g. not playing repeated notes with equal intensity—mostly each second note will need to be a shade lighter (see p.51).

From the first violins you need breadth and varied colours, technical mastery and coordination. Be sure they can see the beat from where they are sitting. Second violins are the rhythmic power-house—this feeling must run right through the section. Then the violas can join in the rhythmic drive. Seek fullness and richness of viola tone. The cellos need to grade the intensity of their sound according to the harmony—in this they will need help. Always be aware of the timing of the double basses—don't let them lag behind. Tell them to beat the cellos to the bow change—the thickness of their strings gives a slightly slower response. Ask for power, clarity and definition in articulation.

With the woodwind and horns, find the balance between coordination and allowing freedom. The character of the beat should also relate to the prominent instrument. The immediacy of the oboes means that they don't need a very sharp beat, but remember that they need more time in their lowest register. See that the flutes blend with the other wind and be aware of their tuning. Be sure that the clarinets are not behind the beat—for them be slightly more definite. Remember that the second bassoon is the foundation of the tuning of the woodwind.

Relate the beat for the horns and brass to the way they breathe—strength in the upbeat, not the downbeat. In order to play quietly, horns need a calm but precise gesture—never show the palm of your hand if they are too loud. Trumpets have a delicate articulation—don't use a large beat. For trombones and tuba, give a slightly faster upbeat, sitting for an instant at the top before coming down. Encourage the brass to master the softer dynamics; look for subtlety and flexibility of tone. Never let the horns sit near the brass—let them relate to the woodwind. Control the dynamics of the wind and brass rather than letting them have their head.

Don't tell the musicians how to play their instruments, but challenge them to produce specific colours and textures of sound. Make simple, brief requests—don't give fanciful explanations. Express by style of beat and rhythmic drive rather than with words. Avoid extreme speeds and above all, let them play—invoking their own awareness and musicality.

PERFORMANCE

In concert, the craft of conducting is the means to interpret the music so, above all, be present. Keep eye contact with the players by not burying your head in the score (see p.38). Avoid extravagant gestures or drifting off into a private Valhalla of inspiration. As the leader, be one step ahead.

Consider the tempo for a moment before beginning a movement and, when beginning, convey the feeling of the rhythm. Such subtleties are shown by the size of beats. They describe both the pulse within the bar and, via first beats, the metre showing the relationship between bars (see p.52–55). The phrases then take shape and connect naturally over the span of a whole movement. Always let the music breathe—the way to this is through breathing calmly and evenly.

The beat also conveys character and dramatic intensity. Here avoid overkill—if overemphatic there is nowhere else to go. Rather, intensity should be carefully graded and built up.

Embrace the whole orchestra; control the dynamics of the wind and brass and entice the strings to produce a rich tone constantly full of character. Keep the double basses up to the beat—unite them with the cellos to make a bass line that drives the harmony.

If the balance between craft and art is found, the players will rise to the occasion. They want to play well but only respond according to the given input. With the right stimulus, they will coordinate and unify. Inspire them and they will contribute in a totally different way. The public will also sense it as the performance takes off.

SUMMARY

To conduct is to be alone with the score. The players trust your interpretation and the public is receptive to it. Without an instrument in the hands, there is no hiding behind glorious tone or brilliant technique—be there just as a musician. If, as an instrumentalist, the score has been a constant companion, your conducting will be empowered.

It is well known that teaching helps your own playing. With the need to explain, a fresh perspective is gained, both in technical and interpretative matters. Constant checks, about practising what is preached, enable you to lead by example. Similarly, there is a two-way connection between playing and conducting, and that is why it is included in this book. If as a conductor you must be a pure musician, describing the depths and subtleties of music, can you be less as a player?

Drawing of Riki Gerardy by Jose Maria de Labra (1975)

AFTERWORD

My appearance on the last page may be like that of a puppeteer coming on stage at the end of the show, or the revelation that a sentient being is operating the computer.

This book has gradually expanded over sixteen years. Thanks are due to the many friends who have offered editorial help and suggestions, also to F. M. Alexander, whose Alexander Technique gives new possibilities to musicians. Certain formative experiences should also be mentioned.

Great music contains magic that can be revealed by the performer who awakens to its content and can transmit the experience. I remember the profundity of Pablo Casals' playing, the mercurial instrumental mastery of Jascha Heifetz and the artistry of Artur Rubinstein. Also, from a distance, the teaching of Nadia Boulanger, who was the equivalent of a magician in perception and recommendation.

Many years were spent trying to understand what I had absorbed. When there is a gap between present abilities and what is known to be possible, the search for missing links continues either consciously or instinctively. Retraining, so that a limitation disappears, can mean being a step nearer an ideal. It is a life journey as well as a musical one—personal growth allows us to see and discover more.

A distinguished teacher, sending his pupil out into the world, told him: 'If you remember 50% of what I have taught you, you will do really well. If you retain 20%, you will still do well but, if you remember 100%, then heaven help you!'

APPENDIX

POINTS OFTEN NEGLECTED

PART ONE—BASICS

STRETCHING.   As our bodies evolved, we were physically active through the struggle for survival. The modern sedentary lifestyle is not natural for us. Physical fitness is essential for a musician. There are many approaches to this, so choose one that is enjoyable.

WALKING.   Contact with the outside world helps to earth us. This is so important, because being alone with an instrument for long periods can be very subjective—daydreams are a hazardous by-product.

POSTURE.   Is it a good idea to bend over the instrument as you play? Good body use is an essential part of the technique of any instrument. Apart from benefit to the player, it will increase communication with an audience. Casals, Heifetz and Rubinstein all had great natural use and it showed in their performances (see p.129).

WARMING UP.   Warm up the creative spirit at the same time as your body, so that time spent practising does not become a purely mechanical process.

BALANCE.   Finding physical balance is a step towards finding inner balance. Learning about how the body works helps in finding range and freedom of movement.

EXERCISES.   Although we may meet a fine player who professes never to practise scales, a starting point for advanced study is the instant ability to produce any scale or arpeggio in any form. The ability to improvise exercises helps solve many technical problems.

CONCEPTION.   There is an obvious advantage for players who study a score away from the instrument, gaining awareness of structure, harmonic background and cultural context. We may learn a degree of musicality at the instrument, but mediocrity is always the danger.

PRODUCTION.   The deeper understanding of the music found by score study needs to be expressed. Be sure that this is happening by not letting the fingers have their own way.

SPONTANEITY.   It is a challenging but essential task to relate knowledge and instinctive feelings. This is a major building block for interpretation.

CONTROL. There is a view that extra body movements enhance our performance. In reality we may, at that moment, be trying to free ourselves from self-induced tension.

FOCUS. Slow practise is the fastest way to make progress. In the competitive world, total accuracy is just the starting point.

DIFFICULTIES. To surmount technical difficulties, the mind needs to slow down to understand the nature of a problem. This can be the hardest of all tasks. From a point of calmness and balance, control can be achieved.

ACCURACY. One stage is to be accurate, another is to make the technique sparkle.

INSPIRATION. By giving constant attention to detail, we are already motivated. Inspiration can then come in its own time.

ROUTINE. Know what you are doing when you practise—it saves so much time. Maintaining full attention may mean practising for shorter periods.

PART TWO—HOMEWORK
PHRASING. This is where much of the magic of music lies.

LINE. Check which phrases need separating—phrasing off is an essential part of musical literacy. Separations also occur within phrases.

INFORMATION. It is not sufficient just to have a vague awareness of the other parts. The score is the source of information.

MELODY. Melodies come alive when there is a balance between planning and spontaneity.

RUBATO. A finely balanced rubato brings out the inner logic of music.

RHYTHM. The most basic element of music. Buoyant rhythms, as in dance music, animate a performance.

PULSE & METRE. The beats in a bar are not equal—see how they relate. See also how the bars relate via their first beat. These subjects are the ones that are generally least known, but they describe what is essential for music to sound right.

HARMONY. Constant awareness of the movement of harmony reveals how the music unfolds.

ARTICULATION. Develop the technique to produce every kind of articulation. Always give attention to the exact type to be used.

DYNAMICS. Work at increasing the dynamic range, especially in performance.

PART THREE—REHEARSAL
RESPONSE & ENSEMBLE. Each line of the music is important—know and relate to them all.

TIMING. If you breathe evenly it will improve your timing. An overview of the work will also help. When playing groups of two quavers or semiquavers (eighth or sixteenth notes) avoid the habit of beginning them late and playing them faster. This style, which can appear to add excitement, often sounds superficial.

TONE. If your basic sound is luscious, where will you go from there? Seek character and colour as well as quality.

INTONATION. This can never be taken for granted.

TECHNIQUE, DETAIL. This is shaping the note to fit the phrase. The ability to play the notes is just the raw material—known as facility.

VIRTUOSITY. Control, quality and flair combine to produce virtuosity.

OBJECTIVITY, LISTENING. Learn to listen to yourself objectively, then much more will be heard.

PART FOUR—BACKGROUND
BACKGROUND. Bring the performance alive by investigating its style and context.

EVOLUTION. Discover different approaches to interpretation by listening to great players of the past, as well as of the present.

STYLE. A sense of style comes from finding the innate character of the music.

EXPRESSION, DRAMA. Find the range by deep examination of content—don't let inhibition limit you.

DEPTH. Put aside superimposition. When approaching a great work, leave yourself out of it—just study its content.

PART FIVE—PERFORMANCE
PREPARATION. To be comfortable performing, know what you are doing and practise doing it in front of people. Project what you know and feel about the music.

MEMORY. A great benefit of harmonic awareness is relative safety if ever the thread of melodic memory is lost. Harmonic memory exists at a deeper level then melodic memory and is less affected by nerves.

NERVES. Breathe calmly and evenly, especially just before a performance.

PACING. It is important to dominate what you are doing—lead the audience rather than follow it.

PART SIX—POST MORTEM
PERSPECTIVE, PROBLEMS. Develop courage to work at those aspects of playing that don't come naturally.

SELF-CONFIDENCE, POISE. Focus on what is being performed, without interfering with the flow of the music.

JUDGEMENT. Develop perception until the way forward becomes clear. This is how to learn to direct your own progress.

Between Music Lessons

How to practise

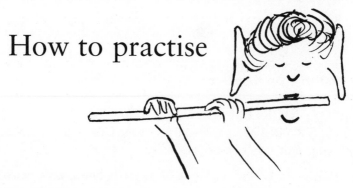

Riki Gerardy
Zelia 2003
ISBN 0-9544675-1-5

This is a book for every young musician. It will show that you are musical and can express it by playing an instrument well.

Illustrated with lots of cartoons, stories and anecdotes, it reveals how to make practice enjoyable. Learn technical skills and every aspect of musicality.

This is a preliminary volume to Beyond the Music Lesson, a handbook for advanced students.

Between Music Lessons *is intended for children. It is entertainingly illustrated in the style of the cartoonist Mel Calman and is full of practical advice for young students of any instrument, from their earliest days onwards. (I enjoyed it a lot and I've just turned seventy.)*

The style is direct, the sentences short and pithy. The subject matter is how music works—the very stuff of music itself!

HUMPHREY BURTON CBE